THE THINKING OF THE SENSIBLE

I0879754

Northwestern University
Studies in Phenomenology
and
Existential Philosophy

Founding Editor †James M. Edie

General Editor Anthony J. Steinbock

Associate Editor John McCumber

THE THINKING OF THE SENSIBLE

Merleau-Ponty's A-Philosophy

Mauro Carbone

Northwestern University Press
Evanston, Illinois

Northwestern University Press
Evanston, Illinois 60208-4210

Copyright © 2004 by Northwestern University Press.
Published 2004. All rights reserved.

Printed in the United States of America

ISBN 0-8101-1363-5 (cloth)
ISBN 0-8101-1986-2 (paper)

Library of Congress Cataloging-in-Publication data are available from the Library of Congress.

The paper used in this publication meets the minimum requirements of the American National Standard for Information Sciences—Permanence of Paper for Printed Library Materials, ANSI Z39.48-1992.

Contents

Abbreviations

Texts by Merleau-Ponty

All references are first to the original French texts, then to the English translations.

"I"

"Un Inédit de Maurice Merleau-Ponty" (1952), *Revue de métaphysique et de morale* 67, no. 4 (1962): 401–9; "An Unpublished Text by Maurice Merleau-Ponty: A Prospectus of His Work," trans. Arleen B. Dallery, in M. Merleau-Ponty, *The Primacy of Perception,* ed. James M. Edie (Evanston: Northwestern University Press, 1964), 3–11.

N

La Nature: Notes, cours du Collège de France, ed. Dominique Séglard (Paris: Seuil, 1995); *Nature: Course Notes from the Collège de France,* trans. Robert Vallier (Evanston: Northwestern University Press, 2003).

NC

Notes des cours au Collège de France 1958–1959 et 1960–1961, ed. Stéphanie Ménasé (Paris: Gallimard, 1996). The notes for the course entitled "Philosophie et non-philosophie depuis Hegel" were previously published (along with the same "Présentation" by C. Lefort that appears in *NC*) in the journal *Textures,* nos. 8–9 (1974): 83–129, and nos. 10–11 (1975): 145–73. These notes appeared in English as "Philosophy and Non-Philosophy Since Hegel," trans. Hugh J. Silverman, in *Philosophy and Non-Philosophy Since Merleau-Ponty,* ed. Hugh J. Silverman (New York and London: Routledge, 1988), 9–83. We make reference to this translation. All English quotations from the other courses have been translated by Romano Ullah Khan and Giacomo Carissimi under our supervision.

OE

L'Oeil et l'esprit (Paris: Gallimard, 1964); "Eye and Mind," trans. Carleton Dallery, improved by Michael B. Smith, in *The Merleau-Ponty*

Aesthetics Reader: Philosophy and Painting, ed. Galen Johnson, translations editor Michael B. Smith (Evanston: Northwestern University Press, 1993), 121–49.

OG

Notes de cours sur "L'Origine de la géométrie" de Husserl, edited by Franck Robert, in Merleau-Ponty, *Notes de cours sur "L'Origine de la géométrie" de Husserl, suivi de recherches sur la phénoménologie de Merleau-Ponty,* under the direction of Renaud Barbaras (Paris: Presses Universitaires de France, 1998), 11–92; *Husserl at the Limits of Phenomenology,* trans. Leonard Lawlor with Bettina Bergo (Evanston: Northwestern University Press, 2001).

PM

La Prose du monde (Paris: Gallimard, 1969); *The Prose of the World,* trans. John O'Neill (Evanston: Northwestern University Press, 1973).

PP

Phénoménologie de la perception (Paris: Gallimard, 1945); *Phenomenology of Perception,* trans. Colin Smith (London: Routledge and Kegan Paul, 1962; revised, 1981).

RC

Résumés de cours: Collège de France, 1952–60 (Paris: Gallimard, 1968); "Themes from the Lecture Courses," trans. John O'Neill, in M. Merleau-Ponty, *In Praise of Philosophy and Other Essays* (Evanston: Northwestern University Press, 1988).

S

Signes (Paris: Gallimard, 1960); *Signs,* trans. Richard McCleary (Evanston: Northwestern University Press, 1964).

SC

La Structure du comportement (Paris: Presses Universitaires de France, 1942); *The Structure of Behavior,* trans. Alden Fischer (Boston: Beacon, 1963).

SNS

Sens et non-sens (Paris: Nagel, 1948); *Sense and Non-Sense,* trans. Hubert Dreyfus and Patricia Dreyfus (Evanston: Northwestern University Press, 1964).

VI

Le Visible et l'invisible (Paris: Gallimard, 1964); *The Visible and the Invisible,* trans. Alphonso Lingis (Evanston: Northwestern University Press, 1968).

Other Texts

PG

G. W. F. Hegel, *Phänomenologie des Geistes* (1807), followed by an indication of the related part or section and the paragraph. Our quotations are drawn from the English translation of Merleau- Ponty's version, which in turn relies on the Kenley Royce Dove translation of Hegel's *Phenomenology of Spirit.* On this subject, see Merleau-Ponty, "Philosophy and Non-Philosophy Since Hegel," trans. Hugh J. Silverman, 297 n. 1 and 300 n. 17. See also *Hegel's Phenomenology of Spirit,* trans. A. V. Miller (New York: Oxford University Press, 1977).

R

M. Proust, *A la recherche du temps perdu,* 3 vols., ed. Pierre Clarac and André Ferré, Bibliothèque de la Pléiade (Paris: Gallimard, 1954); *Remembrance of Things Past* (New York: Vintage, 1981), vol. 1 (trans. C. K. Scott-Moncrieff and Terence Kilmartin), vol. 2 (trans. C. K. Scott-Moncrieff and Terence Kilmartin), vol. 3 (trans. C. K. Scott-Moncrieff, Terence Kilmartin, and Andreas Mayor). Our citations of this work are accompanied by an indication (in Arabic numerals) of the relevant volume.

Preface

In his final writings, Merleau-Ponty confesses to feeling that a "mutation of the relationship between humanity and Being" (*OE* 63/139, trans. modified) is under way in our epoch. He feels, moreover, that there is a need for this mutation.[1] For Merleau-Ponty, this mutation provided the framework for the "new ontology" to which he was hoping to give a full philosophical formulation.

In part, Merleau-Ponty planned to reach this aim by interrogating the philosophical tradition itself. Or rather, *a certain* philosophical tradition: Descartes and Husserl, in particular, but also the authors of what he called "the history of a-philosophy" (*NC* 278/12), starting from Hegel and then continuing on through Marx, Kierkegaard, Nietzsche, and Heidegger. But at the same time, with the same objective in mind, he was exploring other domains: on the one hand, "the evolution of the concept of Nature" (*N* 265/204) and, on the other, the experience of contemporary "poetry, music, painting" (*NC* 46), as well as psychoanalysis. For him, these were "cultural symptoms" (ibid.) through which he perceived the "new ontology" to be *implicitly* at work.

We know how Merleau-Ponty's hope to give a full philosophical *expression* to this ontology was shattered by his untimely death. Still, important fragments of this enterprise exist. One finds them above all in the manuscript and the working notes of *The Visible and the Invisible,* but also in the notes from the courses Merleau-Ponty held during his last years, which continue and—in some respects—go beyond *The Visible and the Invisible.*[2] These fragments are so suggestive that they immediately "mark out a realm to think about" (*S* 202/160), as Merleau-Ponty himself once wrote about Husserl.

The realm that these fragments mark out is that of the questions raised by the enterprise in which Merleau-Ponty felt himself to be engaged. Of these questions, we can say, as Merleau-Ponty did in his discussion of Husserl, that "we can be faithful to and find them only by thinking again" (ibid.). By thinking through these questions again, we can make an attempt to clarify some of the aspects of the "mutation of the relationship between humanity and Being" that Merleau-Ponty confessed to feeling.

Let us first of all ask how Merleau-Ponty pictures this mutated relationship. Perhaps it is best captured, in all its problematic aspects, in a working note of *The Visible and the Invisible* that seeks to define—significantly—the notion of "chiasm." The note reads: "The idea of *chiasm,* that is: every relation with being is *simultaneously* a taking and a being taken, the hold is held, it is *inscribed* and inscribed in the same being that it takes hold of" (*VI* 319/266).

On careful reflection, it seems that it is an idea of just this kind that Merleau-Ponty is looking for in his search through the recesses of the philosophical tradition. And not only there. This definition also effectively characterizes the conception of the relationship between conscious and unconscious that he hopes will definitively affirm itself in psychoanalysis.[3] It likewise appears to be at the heart of the transformations that Merleau-Ponty perceives in contemporary science: "the homogeneity of the measured and the measuring [*mesurant*] implies that the subject makes common cause with space. The idea of an incarnated subject is necessary to understand the microscope and microphysics" (*N* 137/99), he observes with regard to the "philosophical significance of quantum mechanics." Moreover, this definition seems to apply well to the "new bond" (*NC* 190) with the visible that Merleau-Ponty sees as forged in our epoch not only by painting, but also by literature and music.

As is well known, in this panorama of "symptoms," the name of Marcel Proust occupies for Merleau-Ponty a position of sharp relief: "No one has gone further than Proust in fixing the relations between the visible and the invisible, in describing an idea that is not the contrary of the sensible, that is its lining and its depth" (*VI* 195/149). Merleau-Ponty constantly devotes attention to Proust, but in this quote lies the principal reason for his interest in Proust during the final period of his reflections. For a full philosophical formulation of the "new ontology," a different description is necessary of the relationship between the sensible and the intelligible: a new—antiplatonistic—theory of ideas[4] toward which, in Merleau-Ponty's view, Proust has traveled further than any other.

The absolutely central importance that Merleau-Ponty attributes to such a theory in expressing philosophically the "mutation of the relationship between humanity and Being" in our epoch is confirmed by his attempt to employ it even to elaborate "the concept of Nature" today. With this goal in mind, in the second course of his that is dedicated to this topic, he brings up a remarkable convergence between Proust's framework and that of the Goethe-inspired German biologist Jakob von

Uexküll.[5] Merleau-Ponty tries to develop this convergence in order to conceive of the biological notion of "species" as an essence *inseparable* from its manifestation in single individuals—that is, not as a platonistic but rather as a "sensible idea" (*VI* 198/151), not so different from the peculiar idea of love that Proust describes as *inseparable* from the experience of listening to a certain melody.

A theory of ideas naturally implies a theory of their genesis, that is, a theory of ideation. Interestingly, on the very same page in which he brings up the convergence between Proust and Uexküll, Merleau-Ponty identifies a fundamental aspect of the Proustian theory of ideation. He writes: "When we invent a melody, the melody sings itself within us much more than we sing it; it goes down the throat of the singer, as Proust says. . . . [T]he body is suspended in what it sings, the melody incarnates itself and finds in the body a type of servant" (*N* 228/173–174, trans. modified).

It is evident from the passage we have just cited that the Proustian framework revived by Merleau-Ponty conceives of ideation in terms of an attitude that he describes elsewhere—in a Heideggerian manner—in terms of "letting-be":[6] "the melody sings itself within us much more than we sing it," as he emphasizes. The genesis of the idea therefore consists in a kind of *welcoming* that, in turn, gives subjectivity the shape of a "hollow" (*creux*)[7] into which the idea *arrives*, just as the melody *sings itself*.

Here it is important to note that this "hollow" is not a mere *receptacle* of the idea, but rather is essentially united with, is *one and the same as*, the idea's advent: "activity and passivity coupled" (*VI* 314/261), to use the expression of a working note of *The Visible and the Invisible*. Indeed, as Merleau-Ponty explains, to "invent a melody" is for "the melody [to] sing itself within us." In its form of a "hollow," subjectivity thus displays "the passivity of our activity" (*VI* 274/221), of which Merleau-Ponty speaks in another working note of *The Visible and the Invisible* when he emphasizes that to think "is not an *activity* of the soul, nor a production of thoughts in the plural, and I am not even the author of that *hollow* that forms within me by the passage from the present to the retention, it is not I who makes myself think any more than it is I who make my heart beat" (ibid., second emphasis added). In short, in its form of a hollow, subjectivity reveals its own passivity as the *creator* of ideas. Indeed, if the idea is to be described as *arriving* in subjectivity, then that must be because it is *passively created* there.[8] Here we see another decisive antiplatonistic element.

Subjectivity thus conceived is not only the creator of ideas, but also, in a Nietzschean way, the creator of values. As a result, the aesthetic—etymologically linked to the field of perception—implies also the eidetic and the ethical. In the case of these ideas and values, however, subjectivity cannot claim true authorship. Rather, these ideas and values bring to expression the *encounter* of subjectivity with the world, and they find this expression in a "thinking" that operates "without thinking" (*N* 351/283), as Merleau-Ponty writes in one of the final notes of *Nature.* This last remark by Merleau-Ponty leads us to reaffirm that it is the conception of subjectivity as a hollow that pushes him to note the identity of activity and passivity.[9] More than that, it suggests to us that, in the indistinctness of activity and passivity, it is the very being of the encounter with the world that is *reflecting itself.* Or, to put it another way, *thinking itself.*

In this light, perhaps, certain aspects of the "mutation of the relationship between humanity and Being" that Merleau-Ponty noticed begin to take a more precise form—and the mutation seems to consist in having *brought these aspects to expression,* rather than in having *initiated their production.* In fact, given the perspective that this mutation offers, what until now we have continued to call subjectivity—instead of considering the world as an object placed in front of it—*shows* itself rather to be a resonance chamber for our encounter with the *flesh* of the world: "the body is suspended in what it sings, the melody incarnates itself and finds in the body a type of servant."[10] That the world is not reducible to an object is in fact for Merleau-Ponty the first lesson that arises from the study of nature.[11] For this reason, in his view, the study of nature "more clearly shows the necessity of the ontological mutation" (*N* 265/204).

If, in the way in which until now we have described this "mutation of the relationship between humanity and Being," one can discern echoes of Hegel—"that jointing and framing of Being which is being realized through man" (*S* 228/181)—this should not come as a surprise. For in the idea of chiasm, which seems to describe well the relation we have observed between activity and passivity, Merleau-Ponty relocates the intuition according to which Hegel characterizes absolute knowledge as "a knowledge in which . . . savage consciousness and reflected consciousness reciprocate each other" (*NC* 300 n. a/306 n. 54).

This suffices to reveal what it is that Merleau-Ponty feels has been under way "since Hegel," to quote the title of one of his final courses: he is referring to the attempts to formulate the current "mutation of the relationship between humanity and Being" in a framework of thought that, in order to express this mutation, must transform itself from philosophical to *a-philosophical.* "Philosophy has never spoken . . . of the passivity of our activity" (*VI* 274/221), Merleau-Ponty judges. For this reason, he intends to start from the idea of chiasm in order to "elaborate an idea of philosophy" that "cannot be total and active grasp, intellectual possession, since what there is to be grasped is a dispossession" (*VI* 319/266).

From the calling into question of the *frontal positioning* of subject versus object, there can only follow the calling into question of the *grasping* of the object by the subject. The direct result is therefore the calling into question of the modern notion of "concept," the Germanic root of which expresses precisely the intention of grasping. "Philosophy," objects Merleau-Ponty, "is not *above* life, overhanging" (ibid.). Yet from Talete onward, it has traditionally guarded itself against life, treating it as "non-philosophy." To take life into account, recognizing it chiasmatically as *the other side of oneself* rather than as *other than oneself:* in this consists the "idea of philosophy" that Merleau-Ponty also calls "a-philosophy," identifying its principium—in the double sense of initial moment and fundamental notion—in the Hegelian conception of phenomenology.

Philosophy and non-philosophy, then, along with the sensible and the intelligible, subject and object. Couples—encapsulated in the couple of the visible and the invisible—that metaphysics established as oppositional pairs. To revoke this oppositional intention and to declare their mutual belonging; therefore, to mutate philosophy's attitudes and language in order to suit the "mutation of the relationship between humanity and Being" currently in progress: this is the task that Merleau-Ponty glimpsed, that he embarked upon, and that he left open. Given the epochal nature of this task, it could not in any event have been otherwise. But the first steps of this path already determine the direction, and it is in this direction that our book seeks to proceed. It will untangle the connecting strands that we have been outlining in our preface, traversing some of the dialogues that Merleau-Ponty's thinking interweaved in the course of undertaking this task: dialogues, respectively, with the works of Husserl and Proust, of Hegel, of Uexküll, Rimbaud, and again Proust, of Heidegger and—indirectly—Kant. Perhaps in uncovering the reasons and the implications of these interrupted dialogues, this work will on occasion succeed in relaunching the "unthought-of element" (*S* 202/160) of this thinking.

Acknowledgments

I would certainly never have completed this volume without the constant, and friendly, intellectual interchange that was offered to me during these years by Patrick Burke, Leonard Lawlor, and David Michael Levin. More generally, this work owes much to the inspiration and the generosity of Renaud Barbaras, Olivia Custer, Duane H. Davis, Lester Embree, Wayne Froman, Ted Toadvine, and David Wood.

The chapters that make up this book are reworked versions of a number of essays of mine. These essays were translated into English by Elizabeth Locey, Nicoletta Grillo, Romano Ullah Khan, and Giacomo Carissimi, and I am grateful to all of them for their professionalism and their availability. I owe special thanks to Orin Percus for the care and patience with which he helped me to revise the entire text and translated the preface.

"The Time of Half-Sleep: Merleau-Ponty between Husserl and Proust" is the text of a talk that I was invited to present at the International Research Symposium on "Merleau-Ponty's Reading of Husserl," organized jointly by the Center for Advanced Research in Phenomenology and by Florida Atlantic University at Delray Beach, Florida, on November 19–20, 1999. This text, translated by Elizabeth Locey, is included in *Merleau-Ponty's Reading of Husserl,* edited by Ted Toadvine and Lester Embree. Dordrecht: Kluwer Academic Publishers, 2002, 149–72. Copyright © 2002 by Kluwer Academic Publishers. All rights reserved. Reprinted with kind permission from Kluwer Academic Publishers.

An earlier version of "*Ad Limina Philosophiae:* Merleau-Ponty and the 'Introduction' to Hegel's *Phenomenology of Spirit*" was presented, under the title "*Ad Limina Philosophiae:* Merleau- Ponty and the 'Einleitung' to Hegel's *Phänomenologie des Geistes,*" at the annual meeting of the International Symposium on Phenomenology held in Perugia, Italy, on July 17–21, 2000, and dedicated to "The Final Courses Held by Maurice Merleau-Ponty at the Collège de France." That version, translated by Nicoletta Grillo and revised by David Michael Levin, was published in

Chiasmi International, n.s., 3 (2001): 311–27. My thanks to the publishers and the other editors of this journal.

"Nature: Variations on the Theme" is the text of an invited talk that I presented at the XXII Annual International Conference of the Merleau-Ponty Circle, held at Seattle University on September 19–21, 1997, and dedicated to "The Concept of Nature." The text, translated by Romano Ullah Khan and Giacomo Carissimi, has not been published before in its English version.

"The Thinking of the Sensible" is reprinted by permission from *Chiasms: Merleau-Ponty's Notion of Flesh,* edited by Fred Evans and Leonard Lawlor. Albany: State University of New York Press, 2000, 121–30. © State University of New York. All rights reserved. This text, translated by Giacomo Carissimi, is presented here in a revised and somewhat elaborated version.

THE THINKING OF THE SENSIBLE

1

The Time of Half-Sleep: Merleau-Ponty between Husserl and Proust

Lived Time

In the chapter on "The Body as Expression, and Speech" in *Phenomenology of Perception,* Merleau-Ponty cites a famous description of half-sleep given by Marcel Proust in *Remembrance of Things Past:*

> . . . when I awoke like this, and my mind struggled in an unsuccessful attempt to discover where I was, everything revolved around me through the darkness: things, places, years. My body, still too heavy with sleep to move, would endeavor to construe from the pattern of its tiredness the position of its various limbs, in order to deduce therefrom the direction of the wall, the location of the furniture, to piece together and give a name to the house in which it lay. Its memory, the composite memory of its ribs, its knees, its shoulder-blades, offered it a whole series of rooms in which it had at one time or another slept, while the unseen walls, shifting and adapting themselves to the shape of each successive room that it remembered, whirled round it in the dark. . . . [M]y body, the side upon which I was lying, faithful guardians of a past which my mind should never have forgotten, brought back before my eyes the glimmering flame of the night-light in its urn-shaped bowl of Bohemian glass that hung by chains from the ceiling, and the chimney-piece of Siena marble in my bedroom at Combray, in my grandparents' house, in those far-distant days which at this moment I imagined to be in the present without being able to picture them exactly. . . . (*PP* 211 n. 1/181 n. 2)[1]

According to Merleau-Ponty, the experience described on this page from Proust reveals that "memory is, not the constituting consciousness of the past, but an effort to reopen time on the basis of the implications contained in the present" and that "the body, as our permanent means of 'taking up attitudes' and thus constructing pseudo-presents, is the medium of our communication with time as well as with space" (*PP* 211/181, trans. modified). In fact, by virtue of the original movement of intentionality that "produces the natural and antepredicative unity of the world and of our life" (*PP* xiii/xviii), one's own body inhabits a spatiotemporal totality. It animates space and time with its presence, and literally incorporates space and time into its experience, where later it can find their traces.

Thus, far from being an intellectual operation, memory emerges from the corporeal experience of lived space and time. This "body's function in remembering" (*PP* 211/181) appears, therefore, to be at the foundation of what Merleau-Ponty indicates elsewhere as one of the central philosophical ideas of Proust's oeuvre: "the envelopment of the past in the present and the presence of lost time" (*SNS* 45/26).[2]

If we want to penetrate more deeply into the motives behind Merleau-Ponty's interest in Proust's work, our attention is thereby drawn to the analysis of temporality which he develops in the *Phenomenology of Perception*. Concerning this issue, it is also necessary to remember that for Merleau-Ponty "subjectivity, at the level of perception, is nothing but temporality" (*PP* 276/239) because "the spatial synthesis and the synthesis of the object are founded on this unfolding of time" (*PP* 277/239) that one's own body produces. Thus, Merleau-Ponty's reflection endeavors to underline what the description of the waking body in the *Remembrance* has shown: "My body takes possession of time; it brings into existence a past and a future for a present; it is not a thing, but creates time instead of submitting to it" (*PP* 277/240).

How, then, does this time present itself, this time which one's own body "secretes,"[3] as Merleau-Ponty says?

It is precisely this question that Merleau-Ponty chooses to answer in the chapter of *Phenomenology of Perception* dedicated to "Temporality,"[4] in which he is committed to refuting, in its multiple versions, the common notion of time as a "succession of instances of *now*"[5] as well as that of a "non-temporal subject": "The problem is how to make time explicit as it comes into being and makes itself evident [*en train d'apparaître*], time at all times underlying the *notion* of time, not as an object of our knowledge, but as a dimension of our being" (*PP* 475/415).

It is a question of describing the originary experience of time. Merleau-Ponty conceives it as temporality lived by the subject inside his or her own "field of presence,"[6] enclosing these two horizons which, inspired by Husserl, Merleau-Ponty, as we know, calls "horizon of retention" and "horizon of protention." Merleau-Ponty also specifies that what Husserl understands by the notion of retention is not "voluntary memory"—that is, the fruit of intellectual synthesis by which the past event is deliberately evoked—but what we could call the "lived past," which subtends this voluntary memory and which is still retained in the field of presence.[7] Also, as Merleau-Ponty explains in *Phenomenology of Perception:* "when I rediscover the concrete origin of the memory . . . it is, therefore, because I recapture [*rejoins*] time that is lost: because, from the moment in question to my present, the chain of retentions and the interlocking horizons coming one after the other insure an unbroken continuity" (*PP* 478/418). Is it not, then, a question of analyzing, in other terms, "the envelopment of the past in the present and the presence of lost time" that Merleau-Ponty discovers in Proust's work? In fact, Proust's intention is precisely to describe the lived temporality from which Marcel feels the involuntary memory emerge—the involuntary memory which, as Paul Ricoeur emphasizes, "*opens up* the recaptured time."[8]

Merleau-Ponty brings this idea of an implication of the past—and, symmetrically, of the future—in the present to the Husserlian notion of operative intentionality (*fungierende Intentionalität*), that is, to the antepredicative relation which, in unifying the individual with the world, inaugurates lived time. In fact, by virtue of this operative intentionality, which Merleau-Ponty finds again in the Heideggerian concept of transcendence, "[m]y present outruns itself in the direction of an immediate future and an immediate past and impinges upon them where they actually are, namely in the past and in the future themselves" (*PP* 478/418).

This description of the implication of the past and of the future in the present also shows us—in addition to the character of transcendence—the character of continuity in which time is wrapped in our originary experience. Critical of Bergson's thesis on this point, Merleau-Ponty nevertheless affirms that continuity, though it is an "essential phenomenon" (*PP* 481/420), does not however suffice to *explain* time, but calls for clarification in its turn: this continuity must be brought back precisely to the transcendence which pushes the present to surpass itself toward the past and toward the future. In Merleau-Ponty's conception, time thus unfolds itself as a single movement, the different moments of which flow into each other. From this fact, rather than erasing each other, the different moments mutually recall and reaffirm each other—starting from the privileged field of the present[9]—in a sort of coexistence which is habitually hidden by the idea of time as "a succession of instances of *now*." It results from this that time, according to Merleau-Ponty, is one unto itself; and, in his opinion, this is what expresses its "mythical personifications." In this way, in accordance with Proust's tendency to make time a "personified entity," as Ricoeur notes,[10] which will reveal itself more and more as the main character of Proust's work, Merleau-Ponty affirms that "[w]e are not saying that time is *for* someone, which would once more be a case of arraying it out, and immobilizing it. We are saying that time *is* someone, or that temporal dimensions, in so far as they perpetually overlap, bear each other out and ever confine themselves to making explicit what was implied in each, being collectively expressive of that one single explosion or thrust which is subjectivity itself" (*PP* 482–83/422).

The circularity of temporal dimensions comes to light in this manner in lived temporality, a circularity analogous to that which Florival notes in Proust's work: "the past is realized through the future that reveals and unfolds all of its possibilities. A past, the presentness [*l'actualité*] of which had not been recognized in its time, looms up in the light of present temporality. Thus, the reversibility of time is finally obtained."[11] It is probably this manner of posing the problem which allows Merleau-Ponty to not see the opposition between the "intermittences" of Proustian time and his own phenomenological conception of temporal continuity.

But the circularity of temporal dimensions inside of lived temporality cannot be understood if one conceives of ultimate subjectivity (where there is the consciousness of time) as "intratemporal," that is—in Heideggerian terms—as an "innerworldly being" (*innerweltliches Seiendes*) which is arrayed out *in* time.[12] In this case, in fact, temporal dimensions could present themselves only as reciprocally antagonistic, because it would be impossible for an irremediably intratemporal subjectivity to develop the cohesion among these dimensions which makes their relation circular. This does not, however, situate subjectivity in a sort of eternity. Merleau-Ponty, on the contrary, emphasizes that "we must understand time as the subject and the subject as time" (*PP* 483/422). In this chiasm, the two formulas clarify each other mutually. The first intends to indicate that the "object time" or "constituted time" of intratemporality (that is, time as a "succession of instances of *now*" or as a "developed series of presents") is made possible precisely by the "subject time" or "constituting time" that presents itself "as an indivisible thrust and transition" (*PP* 484/423); it subtends object time and coagulates into it. In return, the second formula aims to underline the fact that subjectivity, insofar as it is enrooted in a field of presence, expresses its own "indivisible power" in "distinct [i.e., intratemporal] manifestations," but at the same time—from the fact of the movement of transcendence which characterizes it as temporality—it does not cease to recapture these manifestations in developing their coexistence and circularity.

In this duality, Merleau-Ponty sees a light bursting forth: that of the *"relationship of self to self"* (*PP* 487/426). He then continues by affirming that "it is through temporality that there can be, without contradiction, ipseity, significance and reason" (*PP* 487/426).

The duality of the phenomenon that we have just described is expressed in the concept of temporalization, which designates the movement by which lived time springs forth: the subject finds itself *situated* in this movement (of which it is not the author), but can at the same time *take on* this situation. Thus, Merleau-Ponty considers that the concept of temporalization makes possible the elucidation of the paradox that Husserl calls the "passive synthesis" of time.

Time and Subject

Fifteen years after the publication of *Phenomenology of Perception,* in April 1960, Merleau-Ponty drafted one of the most dense and most pregnant working notes of *The Visible and the Invisible*—entitled "'Indestructible' Past, and intentional analytic—and ontology"—beginning with the following words:

> The Freudian idea of the unconscious and the past as "indestructible," as "intemporal" = elimination of the common idea of time as a "series of *Erlebnisse*"—There is an architectonic past. cf. Proust: the *true* hawthorns are the hawthorns of the past—Restore this life without *Erlebnisse,* without interiority . . . which is, in reality, the "monumental" life, *Stiftung,* initiation.
>
> This "past" belongs to a mythical time, to the time before time, to the prior life, "farther than India and China"—(*VI* 296/243)

By this exordium, Merleau-Ponty expresses his intention of rethinking the Husserlian description of time—and, consequently, the themes of the continuity of time and subjectivity as temporality—in supplying the ontology of brute sensible being with motifs of reflection drawn once again from Proust's *Remembrance,* as well as Freudian psychoanalysis.

In fact, the "ontological rehabilitation of the sensible" (*S* 210/167) that Merleau-Ponty had announced in "The Philosopher and His

Shadow"[13] also has consequences for the conception of time and subjectivity, and ends by bringing Merleau-Ponty to criticize the way in which Husserl himself treats these problems.

As another working note from *The Visible and the Invisible* affirms, "[t]he sensible, Nature, transcend the past present distinction, realize from within a passage from one into the other Existential eternity" (*VI* 321/267).[14] The dimension of the *erste Natur* which underlies the concept of Nature that dominates beginning with Descartes is, in other words, the dimension of the *erste Geschichtlichkeit,* in which palpitates a time that is not "the serial time, that of 'acts' and decisions" (*VI* 222/168), but rather a time characterized by the enjambment of simultaneity "upon succession and diachronics" (*S* 154/123).[15] It deals with the time that Merleau-Ponty now calls precisely "mythical": a time, he explains, "where certain events 'in the beginning' maintain a continued efficacity" (*VI* 43/24).[16]

But the ontological rehabilitation of the sensible does not limit itself to transcending the distinction between past and present; it also leads us back to this side of the distinction between time and space. The sensible, in fact—as an indivisible stuff which interweaves things, animals, and others at the same time as our body—opens us to them in a simultaneity which is just as much temporal as spatial, as the innovations of contemporary painting have revealed. And the sensible makes the latency of the elsewhere, as well as that of past and future, erupt in the here and now, as happens to Marcel with the rediscovered hawthorns.[17]

Merleau-Ponty emphasizes that our perceptual opening to Being is, thus, the "foundation of space *and of time*" (*VI* 244/191, Merleau-Ponty's emphasis): it is to this that the concept of *Stiftung,* evoked in the working note cited at the beginning of this section, alludes.

In its turn, this Husserlian concept refers to that of "institution," which Merleau-Ponty had introduced in his writings in the first half of the 1950s to indicate how sense is not constituted by consciousness but autoconstitutes itself inside of a system that is structured diacritically.[18] It is precisely according to this acceptation that Merleau-Ponty now defines time—but he conceives of space in the same fashion—as "an institution, a system of equivalences" (*VI* 238/184) whose sense is not constituted by our intentional activity, as *Phenomenology of Perception* had already shown, but autoconstitutes itself, as Merleau-Ponty now adds, inside the carnal fabric of differentiations *of which we are* [*dont nous "en sommes"*]. As seeing-visibles, we are in fact inherent in a visible present which, all the while inhabiting us, announces and opens up to us simultaneously other invisible dimensions of space and time, compossibles insofar as they are all levied against Being as "universal dimensionality" (*VI* 289/236). As Merleau-Ponty implies more than once, it is thus on the model of the ontology of the visible that this fabric of spatiotemporal differentiations should be described.[19] What in fact does simultaneity indicate, if not the chiasm of presence and absence sketched by the relation between visible and invisible? And how, then, does the relation—on which the institution feeds—between the sedimented presence of the instituted element and the latency of possibilities of the instituting element appear, except as the chiasmic relation between visible and invisible?[20]

It is precisely in understanding "time as chiasm" (*VI* 321/267), one of the working notes from *The Visible and the Invisible* tells us, that we can understand that "past and present are *Ineinander*, each enveloping-enveloped" (*VI* 321/268), without having to attribute to time the "essential phenomenon" (*PP* 481/420) of continuity, which was by contrast affirmed in *Phenomenology of Perception*. Thus, the ontological perspective drafted in the final writings pushes Merleau-Ponty to "take up again, deepen, and rectify"[21] his own earlier conception of time—to which elsewhere the ontological perspective is in part beholden[22]—and consequently pushes him to move farther away from the description given of it by Husserl.

Our carnal opening to the world is for Merleau-Ponty, in brief, the *Urstiftung* of a *Zeitpunkt* and of a *Raumpunkt* which inaugurates a diacritical system of temporal and spatial indices, a "*spatializing-temporalizing vortex* (which is flesh and not consciousness facing a noema)" (*VI* 298/244, emphasis added)—as he explains, precisely by critiquing Husserl, in the working note by which we started this section.[23]

Merleau-Ponty is led to this critique of Husserl by, among other things, the deepening of his reflection on the phenomenon of memory, which was linked in *Phenomenology of Perception* to that of temporal continuity. There, however, Merleau-Ponty failed to see a contradiction—as we have already noted—between that conception and the analysis of the "intermittences of the heart" by means of which Proust shows discontinuity, on the contrary, to be a characteristic aspect of the functioning of memory.[24]

In a working note from *The Visible and the Invisible,* Merleau-Ponty now concentrates precisely on the "problem of forgetting," which "lies essentially in the fact that it is discontinuous" (*VI* 248/194),[25] and consequently constitutes an obstacle for a philosophy of consciousness. For Merleau-Ponty, it is this essential discontinuity that the diagram of retentions and protentions formulated by Husserl—taken up by Merleau-Ponty on his own account in the chapter on "Temporality" in

Phenomenology of Perception—no longer seems able to offer an account of. This is because, in spite of Husserl's efforts, the diagram still presupposes "the convention that one can represent the series of nows by points on a line" (*VI* 248/195).

Several lines further, Merleau-Ponty nevertheless specifies that he does not intend to critique Husserl from a Bergsonian point of view for having "spatialized" time: we have seen, in fact, that it is the very distinction between space and time which, in his opinion, is called into question in the horizon of brute being. Instead, the critique that Merleau-Ponty addresses to Husserl is that of not having seen what Merleau-Ponty prefers now to define as the "vortex" of our temporalization-spatialization—that is, our field of presence—in its gestaltist form. By placing transcendence in relief, in fact, this form can account for the discontinuous aspects of that field, or better, surpass the very opposition between continuity and discontinuity precisely in the figure-ground model. It thereby shows forgetting, just with its discontinuous character, as "a manner of being to . . . in turning away from . . . " (*VI* 251/196), that is, as the reverse of memory, precisely according to the gestaltist relation which links the visible and the invisible, a relation in which the first term implicates differentiation and the second dedifferentiation.[26]

As another working note from *The Visible and the Invisible* explains, Merleau-Ponty critiques Husserl for having conceived of the field of presence "as without thickness, as immanent consciousness" while, from his perspective, he unceasingly emphasizes that "it is transcendent consciousness, it is being at a distance" (*VI* 227/173) precisely by virtue of its gestaltist form. It is indeed by virtue of this form that, in our field of presence, the present sketches itself simultaneously with the past to which it obliquely refers, and that, consequently, the reminiscence of this past does not presuppose the intervention of an intentional act. According to Merleau-Ponty, Husserl's conception, on the contrary, cannot account for this simultaneity of past and present, because the intentional analytic—on which this conception rests—"tacitly assumes a place of absolute contemplation *from which* the intentional explicitation is made, and which could embrace present, past, and even openness toward the future" (*VI* 297/243).[27] In this fashion, Husserl's conception gives, about the past, not a "vertical" vision, in which it gives itself simultaneously with the present, but a "surveying" vision, in the sense of a vision from the perspective of this "place of absolute contemplation" starting from which consciousness, across the series of its intentional acts, supports the continuity of temporal dimensions. This conception, "blocked by the framework of *acts* which imposes upon it the philosophy of *consciousness*" (*VI* 297/244), finishes then, according to Merleau-

Ponty, as we have seen in the note cited at the opening of this section, by revealing itself still subordinate to a serial idea of time. It is so precisely insofar as it refers to the order of consciousness conceived as a *series* of intentional acts, which present the link between past and present as adhesion of the consciousness of the past to the consciousness of the present, and not as their *Ineinander* being, precisely not as simultaneity. According to Merleau-Ponty, what underlies Husserl's conception is consequently "an ontology that obliges whatever is not nothing to *present* itself to the *consciousness* across *Abschattungen* and as deriving from an originating donation which is an *act,* i.e., one *Erlebnis* among others" (*VI* 298/244). Merleau-Ponty, on the other hand, emphasizes that "it is necessary to take as primary, not the consciousness and its *Ablaufsphänomen* with its distinct intentional threads, but," as we have already seen, "the spatializing-temporalizing vortex (which is flesh and not consciousness facing a noema)" (*VI* 298/244). In other words, this vortex refers not to the intentional activity of consciousness, but to "the *fungierende or latent* intentionality which is the intentionality within being" (*VI* 297–98/244).

In examining the concept of temporality in *Phenomenology of Perception,* we have already noted how Merleau-Ponty saw operative intentionality as the antepredicative relation between the world and our life, a relation which precisely inaugurates lived time, and how he assimilated the Husserlian notion of operative intentionality to the Heideggerian notion of transcendence, putting it at the base of his own analysis of temporality. But operative intentionality was then still conceived within the "'consciousness'—'object' distinction" (*VI* 253/200) from which this work started, as a working note from *The Visible and the Invisible* indeed recognizes, and consequently appeared to be marked by a duality between activity and passivity. It is precisely this "duality" (in Merleau-Ponty's words) which the concept of temporalization expressed in describing the subject, on the one hand, as plunged into the movement of time, and, on the other hand, as able to take on the sense of this movement and to have the experience of its continuity by virtue of its own transcendence. In short, by means of this transcendence, the present could *surpass itself* toward the past and toward the future, whereas we have now seen Merleau-Ponty demonstrating the simultaneity in which the temporal dimensions sketch themselves within the field of presence.

The descent, in the footsteps of Husserl, into our "archeological" domain, and the ontological rehabilitation of the sensible which has followed it, therefore have not remained without consequences—just as "The Philosopher and His Shadow" shows—for the "conception of noesis, noema, and intentionality" (*S* 208/165).[28] In revealing the indivisible dimension of the inaugural *there is* [*il y a*], this research has in fact shown that "the constituting consciousness is the philosopher's professional imposter" (*S* 227/180). At the same time, the linked meditation on *Gestalttheorie* and on Saussure's linguistics has paved a way into Merleau-Ponty's thought for the idea of transcendence as divergence [*écart*]. He manages to develop this idea into an ontological perspective by seeing in the very structure of Being the source of that transcendence and by indicating in that divergence the latent sense which is sketched in the dimension of the *there is*.[29] The sense which precedes the face-to-face of consciousness and the object, the distinction between activity and passivity, is autoconstituted precisely by virtue of the operative intentionality internal to Being itself. The intimate relationship which links this conception of intentionality with the structural idea of sense as autoproduction of a diacritically organized system is clarified in this way. Thus Merleau-Ponty's thought frees itself from the influence of the philosophy of consciousness. We can, in fact, measure the distance which separates this conception from that of *Phenomenology of Perception:* if the preface of this work affirmed that operative intentionality furnishes "the text which our knowledge tries to translate into precise language" (*PP* xiii/xviii)—thus recalling the conception of unreflective consciousness as positive foundation—sense animated by operative intentionality presents itself now as the divergence which cuts across the sensible being *of which we are.*[30]

Thus conceived, Merleau-Ponty consequently explains, operative intentionality "becomes the thread that binds, for example, my present to my past in its temporal place, such as it was (and not such as I reconquer it by an *act* of evocation)" (*VI* 227/173).

It is therefore in developing the notion of operative intentionality in this ontological perspective that Merleau-Ponty intends to "leave the philosophy of *Erlebnisse* and to pass to the philosophy of our *Urstiftung*" (*VI* 275/221) and hence to show "the passivity of our activity" (*VI* 274/221). Actually, we have seen that the "philosophy of *Erlebnisse*" attributes the constitution of our system of retentions and protentions to the intentional activity of consciousness. What emerges, on the contrary, in the philosophy of spatiotemporal *Urstiftung* which inaugurates our field of presence, according to Merleau-Ponty, is not only that we do not constitute time but that our retentions themselves do not refer back to an intentional act of consciousness. Rather, they refer precisely to the operative intentionality internal to Being.

Consequently, this conception modifies that of subjectivity as temporality affirmed in *Phenomenology of Perception.* While in fact confirming that "time is thus myself" (*S* 231/184), as Merleau-Ponty writes in a manner which makes evident the aspects of Bergson's philosophy present in his own thought,[31] this conception also indicates that I am not "a flux of individual *Erlebnisse*" but "a field of Being" (*VI* 293/240) structured according to the model of the visual field. This field is composed of dimensional differences which are cut out on the universal dimensionality of Being. Even self-presence is sketched, therefore, in diacritical terms: in fact, it cannot be coincidence with the lived, because the visible present is not without its invisible ground.[32] This coincidence therefore can only be, as Merleau-Ponty affirms by means of an expression that comes precisely from Bergson in the lines we have just cited in a footnote, "partial coincidence" insofar as it gives itself as "coinciding from afar" (*VI* 166/125).[33] In this sense, Merleau-Ponty writes that "Self-presence . . . is an *absence from oneself,* a contact with the Self *through* the divergence [*écart*] with regard to Self—The figure on a ground" (*VI* 246/192, trans. modified). It is here that Merleau-Ponty's self-criticism relative to the concept of the tacit Cogito, which precisely tried to indicate being close to oneself in primordial and silent experience, is enrooted. And it is also here that the conception of subjectivity as "*fissure,*" which already appeared in *Phenomenology of Perception* without being deepened, is developed.[34] In *The Visible and the Invisible,* Merleau-Ponty emphasizes that subjectivity is "*fissure,*" not in the Sartrean sense of pure nothingness, of an emptiness or "hole" immediately filled with the plenitude of being, but in the sense of a "hollow," hollowed out precisely by the woof of sensible being's differentiations. In fact, this woof culminates by folding itself back into a sensible which, on the other side—the side of absence of its presence to that being, the "spiritual side" spoken of by Husserl—is also sensing.[35] By virtue of this, therefore, the sensible-sensing sketches a hollow inside the sensible by which the reflexivity of this very sensible exerts itself.

In light of the foregoing, we can now see what Merleau-Ponty calls the "passivity of our activity." As a field of differentiations cut across by the transcendence of Being, the one which we can no longer properly call "subject," in his dealings with the flesh of the world in which he is held, participates in the looming up of sense at the heart of Being. In other words, in these dealings animated by latent intentionality, perception *accomplishes itself* in the indistinction between perceiving and being perceived. Consciousness does not consist, therefore, in operating a series of acts of attribution of sense, but reveals itself as "transcendence, as to be surpassed by . . . and hence as ignorance" (*VI* 250/197). In this sense, our activity is always doubled with a passivity, and what Merleau-Ponty calls "the second and more profound sense of narcissism" (*VI* 183/139) is the narcissism of Being itself: the reflexivity by virtue of which it manifests *itself.* Merleau-Ponty again makes allusion to all of this in the working note of *The Visible and the Invisible* dedicated to the problem of forgetting: he emphasizes that what must be affirmed is "that the things have us, and that it is not we who have the things. That the being that has been cannot stop having been. The 'Memory of the World.' That language has us and that it is not we who have language. That it is being that speaks within us and not we who speak of being" (*VI* 247/194).

As one of the working notes by which we began this section suggested in other terms, Being announces itself at the same time as always *already there* before us and as always "at the first day": it is for this reason that the time that palpitates in this dimension marks precisely the passivity of our activity.[36] In fact, still commenting on Bergson's thought, Merleau-Ponty writes that "I know my duration as no one else does because *I am caught up in it;* because *it overflows me,* I have an experience of it which could not be more narrowly or closely conceived" (*S* 231/184, emphasis added).

This time, this duration which I am insofar as *I am of* brute being, always already there and always at the first day—as this same essay emphasizes—is a time "always new and, precisely in this respect, always the same" (*S* 231/184). Consequently, this time outlines a sort of "existential eternity," the simultaneity between past and present. It deals with the "mythical time" about which we have seen Merleau-Ponty evoke the names of Proust and Freud, this time which he opposes to serial time and in the conception of which the critique of the modern category of *novum* comes to the surface.

The last of *The Visible and the Invisible* working notes to which we have made allusion designates the time which palpitates in the dimension of brute being as "a sort of time of sleep" (*VI* 320/267).[37] In sleep, as in the dimension of brute being, where subject and object are not yet constituted, where activity and passivity are undifferentiated, where space and time lose their distinction, the present is enveloped, in fact, by a past which is the farthest away, a past defined by the citation with which we began this section as "indestructible," as "intemporal." It is precisely the past evoked in this citation that Merleau-Ponty sees brought to the surface by the "associations" used by Freudian psychoanalysis.[38]

With respect to this past, this same note invokes "the Proustian corporeity as guardian of the past" (*VI* 297/243) against the order of consciousness which blocks the Husserlian analysis of temporality. Already in *Phenomenology of Perception,* the influence of Proust on the Merleau-Pontian analysis of temporality seemed to temper that of Husserl and led Merleau-Ponty, as we have already indicated, to accentuate, in comparison to Husserl, "the body's function in remembering." Now, the lesson of Proust on this subject seems to assert itself decidedly in comparison to that of Husserl. In fact, because it is through the body that we are implicated in brute sensible being, according to an indistinction between activity and passivity, the body presents itself as the guardian of "mythical time," of the "existential eternity" which palpitates in brute sensible being. This seems to be alluded to in the concise passage from a working note of *The Visible and the Invisible* which clearly intends to emphasize the identity of activity and passivity, a passage in which Merleau-Ponty announces his intention to "[p]osit the existential eternity—the eternal body" (*VI* 318/265). And if, as was already the case in *Phenomenology of Perception,* this eternity seems to be enrooted in temporality—it makes itself one only with "mythical" time—nevertheless, unlike *Phenomenology of Perception,* the power to "eternalize" is here no longer a privilege of speech.[39] Instead, sedimentation is defined as a synonym "of secondary passivity, that is, of *latent* intentionality" (*VI* 227/173). In short, sedimentation gives itself by virtue of our spatiotemporal *Urstiftung* in Being, and it is precisely the notion of *Urstiftung* that we have seen Merleau-Ponty oppose to the "philosophy of *Erlebnisse*" with the aim of showing the passivity of our activity. The preface to *Signs* seems to refer us to this conception when, paraphrasing Proust's allusion to the figure of "embodied time,"[40] Merleau-Ponty affirms that "I function by construction. I am installed on a pyramid of time which has been me" (*S* 21/14).[41] The figure of "embodied time" and Proust's work in its entirety, in fact, describe a life without reflective consciousness, an experience emerging precisely as in sleep or in one of those states of half-sleep of which the *Remembrance* is full[42] and of which we saw a famous example, cited in *Phenomenology of Perception,* at the beginning of this chapter. In short, the object of Proust's search [*recherche*] is this "life without *Erlebnisse,* without interiority" (*VI* 296/243) that Merleau-Ponty also intends "to restore." In this manner, both of them profoundly show the disintegration of the very notion of the subject[43] and, thereby, the consequent "mutation of the relationship between humanity and Being" (*OE* 63/139, trans. modified) within which we are living.

2

Ad Limina Philosophiae: Merleau-Ponty and the "Introduction" to Hegel's *Phenomenology of Spirit*

"La vraie philosophie se moque de la philosophie, est aphilosophie": "true philosophy scoffs at philosophy, since it is a-philosophical" (*NC* 275/9). It is in this way—paraphrasing Pascal[1]—that Merleau-Ponty formulates the terms of his problematization of philosophy at the beginning of one of the two courses at the Collège de France that he was teaching at the time of his sudden death. The course, entitled "Philosophy and Non-Philosophy Since Hegel," suggests another way to think about the "mutation of the relationship between humanity and Being" that Merleau-Ponty feels in our epoch.

The concept of "non-philosophy," unlike that of "a-philosophy," does not appear for the first time on this occasion in Merleau-Ponty's thought. In fact, it already appears in the preparatory notes and in the *résumé* of the course held in 1958–59,[2] where it turns up as the very theme of his reflections on "the possibility of philosophy today" (*RC* 141/167). In a similar way, in the contemporaneous working notes for the book that will afterward be called *The Visible and the Invisible,*[3] that concept seems to synthesize Merleau-Ponty's judgment regarding our present time, thereby giving definition to the reason and the features of that book.

Nevertheless, in the preparatory notes for the course entitled "Philosophy and Non-Philosophy Since Hegel," this latter concept seems to change with regard to the meaning and the connotation we just recalled. Earlier, in fact, it meant, in a general way, our philosophical condition of "crisis" and "ruin" and, more precisely, "a certain modern obscurity, a pure interrogation" in which Merleau-Ponty found the "sole common denominator" (*RC* 144/170) for the authors coming *after Hegel.*[4] Now—despite what the title of the course may suggest—that concept helps to describe "something" that *began* with Hegel and continued with Marx, Kierkegaard, Nietzsche, and Heidegger.[5] This concept deals with the various attempts, following one another, to build a philosophy finally able to establish and maintain a close connection with what was, on the contrary, traditionally devalued: what is "on this side," namely "appearance," "existence," "life," and "experience"—in short, "non-philosophy," a philosophy able to open a negative way to Being[6] precisely through "non-philosophy," understood here not as the opposite of philosophy itself, but rather as its reverse: a philosophy that would become, in a word, "a- philosophy."

What Beginning of Knowledge?

According to Merleau-Ponty, then, it was Hegel who opened the way for those moments of "the history of a-philosophy" (*NC* 278/12), because in the *Phenomenology of Spirit* he stated the principle according to which "one attains the absolute by way of a phenomenology (the appearance of mind; mind in the phenomenon) . . . because the absolute would not be absolute if it did not appear as absolute" (*NC* 275/9). Thus, the first and more important part of these preparatory notes by Merleau-Ponty, the part we will be considering (the other analyzes some of young Marx's texts), comments on the pages of Hegel's "Introduction" ("Einleitung") to the *Phenomenology of Spirit* which Merleau-Ponty read as reproduced in Heidegger's essay *Hegels Begriff der Erfahrung*[7]—and, in particular, on the last paragraphs of the "Introduction," designated, according to Heidegger's division, with numbers thirteen to sixteen.[8]

As we know, the focus of those pages—pages that, as Merleau-Ponty points out, were not yet indicated as the "Introduction" in the first edition of the work, and were without any title[9]—is the problem of the relation between knowledge and the absolute. We also know, on the basis of some hints much earlier than the first of his working notes, that precisely the problem of knowledge—and in particular the problem of the passage from the realm of the sensible to that of intellectual knowledge—should have taken a central position in *The Visible and the Invisible.* Nevertheless, the manuscript of this last work, after reconsidering the theme of primordial "perceptual faith" from an ontological perspective, stops before treating directly that passage, but not without having characterized it significantly as a "surpassing that does not leave its field of origin" (*VI* 200/153). Merleau-Ponty's confrontation with these pages from Hegel accordingly emerges from the intricate reflections he undertakes on this problem, reflections that would undergo major developments in the work the philosopher was preparing.

On the other hand, this confrontation, and in a larger sense the whole of these preparatory notes, contribute in their turn to delineate more clearly the outlines of the "idea of philosophy"[10]—or better, the idea of "a-philosophy"—to which these developments would arrive, motivated by the need for "truly recasting" the conception of knowledge "according to [its] contact with our life. We must take science within us in its nascent state" (*NC* 282/15).

Now, the principle that Merleau-Ponty recognizes as the basis of Hegel's phenomenology shows that this very "science in its nascent state," since it is the *Erscheinung* of *Wissen*, its *phainesthai*, is the "spot" that intellectual knowledge "surpasses" without leaving it, the "spot" from which it "ascends," to use another even more meaningful expression from Merleau-Ponty—and shows that this "ascent at the spot" (*VI* 231/177) does not configure the concept of knowledge, in accordance with the metaphysical tradition, as approaching the truth from the outside: in fact, we are always already in the truth because of the presence of the absolute to ourselves: the absolute that to Hegel is at one with the truth.

"From the beginning, the absolute: 'was already in and for itself close to us of its own accord' [*an und für sich schon bei uns wäre*]" (*NC* 296/30). Merleau-Ponty stresses these words. If the absolute were not already close to us from the very beginning, how could we possibly know it? In this way, the decisive importance of the beginning, of the "origin of truth,"[11] becomes clearer, since we see that, as it is reaffirmed here, "the 'birth' of truth is not the movement to another *Seiende*" (*NC* 313 n. a/309 n. 72), given the identity of the absolute and truth. But does not this identity—Merleau-Ponty asks—mean perhaps "a dogmatic leap into the absolute" (*NC* 281/15)? No, he says, not if this identity is understood as "*Weltthesis:* the identity of our being and knowing" (ibid.), in the sense—as explained by "The Philosopher and His Shadow"—"of a primordial faith and a fundamental and original opinion (*Urglaube, Urdoxa*)" (*S* 207/163), charged with that insuperable truth with which *The Visible and the Invisible,* literally, *begins:* "We see the things themselves, the world is what we see" (*VI* 17/3).

In precisely that sense, the beginning of knowledge is to be found in common opinion, in the doxa of the natural attitude that in reality is an *Urdoxa,* and thus in *Erfahrung* as "openness" (*NC* 292/26) to the world. Thus, Hegel's shadow converges with that of Husserl[12] in showing to Merleau-Ponty's research the "spot" from which it would be possible "to take another point of departure" (*VI* 67/43), that place which indicates the ontological features of phenomenology and implicitly proposes it as an "a-philosophy." And, as Merleau-Ponty in fact notes: "Phenomenology is this self-presentation of mind, an appearance which is not an effect of the absolute, but the absolute itself. In that respect, philosophy is experience" (*NC* 282/15). In this way, he raises the problem of "the relation between phenomenology and absolute knowledge (metaphysics)" (*NC* 285/19).[13]

As we already said, the confrontation with Hegel developed in the notes we are considering can allow us to focalize in a better way the idea of philosophy—or a-philosophy—that Merleau-Ponty planned to elaborate in *The Visible and the Invisible.* As is well known, in the manuscript of this work, he formulates, in regard to that idea, the concept of *hyper-reflection* (*surréflexion*), polemicizing against the philosophy of reflection. This philosophy seems to him nourished by the conviction that it can explain, by reflection, everything that is implicit in our unreflected life, because what is found in the unreflected would have been put there by the Cogito itself, and therefore the operations of reflection would not imply any modification but only a conversion of the unreflected into its truth.[14] Thus, if reflective analysis tends to bring non-philosophy back to philosophy and to reduce it to philosophy, hyper-reflection attempts to be a philosophical prolongation of non-philosophy, that is, a continuous and conscious renewal of the *same* "by other means" (*VI* 190 n. */145 n. 5), in order to give it a voice.

Against the philosophical framework according to which reflection, on the one hand, presupposes perceptual faith and, on the other, refuses to acknowledge its irreducible priority, Merleau-Ponty supports an idea of philosophy that, according to the concept of hyper-reflection, could account for the "total situation"—that is, the reciprocity between the two terms of that relation[15]—"by admitting the double polarity of reflection and by admitting that, as Hegel said, to retire into oneself is also to leave oneself" (*VI* 74/49).[16]

This phrase from Hegel is one of the *petites phrases* we can often read in Merleau-Ponty's texts, where they come to connote and, in a way, to summarize some especially important passages of his thought. Even in an analysis without any claims to being exhaustive, we can often encounter this phrase. It returns in *The Visible and the Invisible,* always in contrast to reflective philosophy, marking the unreflected and reflection in their co-originality and circularity.[17] These are the traits of the hyper-reflection we already sketched. Moreover, this same phrase also qualifies genuinely "dialectical thought" (*VI* 124/89), reaffirms "the identity . . . of the lived through with the distance" (*VI* 165/124), describes reflection as "rending" (*VI* 233/179), and finally defines the "chiasm" or the "reversal" with regard to which "true philosophy" has the task of apprehending what really renders it so.[18]

In the preparatory notes we are considering, that phrase from Hegel is again echoed in order to designate the chiasm[19] and, in the immediately preceding page, to outline the nature of absolute knowledge.[20]

Thus, this short review shows how in Merleau-Ponty's conception "true philosophy," dialectically modulated because it is founded on hyper-reflection as a reflection that is in a consciously chiasmic relation with the unreflected, is called upon to "apprehend what makes" the chiasm of the interior and the exterior. At the same time, this very review shows how such a configuration of "true philosophy" is for Merleau-Ponty connected to the configuration of absolute knowledge that he sees emerging in the "Introduction" to the *Phenomenology of Spirit*.

In fact, in his commentary on the thirteenth and fourteenth paragraphs of this text, Merleau-Ponty seems to find there some essential aspects of the ontology he was elaborating at that time,[21] starting from how experience takes shape for the "natural consciousness," that is, starting from the theme of the beginning of knowledge.

This experience—in which, little by little, consciousness sees in its vanishing what it had considered to be the "in itself" and thus discovers instead that this was so only *for consciousness itself,* while in the meantime a new object to which a new knowledge is related appears to it—is qualified by Hegel as a "*dialectical* movement, which consciousness exercises on itself—on its knowledge as well as its object— . . . , *in so far as the new, true object emerges to consciousness.*"[22]

Merleau-Ponty comments that only this experience "can make way for a dialectic, because it alone—as we announced—is an openness" (*NC* 292/26) to a transcendent, and because this "relation to a transcendent" is in the meantime relation to the self: a simultaneous reference of consciousness—in its *Zweideutigkeit*—to both of them, that is, a "latent intentionality [that] calls for reversals and not dependence in the unitary sense direction of a noema in relation to a noesis" (ibid.). In experience so conceived, indeed, the latent intentionality guarantees, between those two relations, a reversibility of the roles between the "measured" (*mesuré*) and the "standard of measurement" (*mesurant*); and that reversibility "makes the apprenticeship of consciousness and the appearance of knowledge possible—leads immediately to a relation with the absolute" (*NC* 300/35), because "the absolute is the reversal of roles between the measured and the standard of measurement" (*NC* 289/22). Again, by virtue of this reversibility, knowledge changes itself just as the object does,[23] thanks to "the interdependent notions of the active and the passive" which, according to Merleau-Ponty, the philosophies of reflection are not capable of conceiving in that way.[24] And the truth, instead of sparkling in the coincidence of the one with the other, shines—ambiguously—only through their "exchange" (*NC* 303/38).[25]

Thus, in the Hegelian *Erfahrung* Merleau-Ponty sees the outlines of that "vertical world"[26] of which he planned to formulate the ontological sense in *The Visible and the Invisible.* In the *Zweideutigkeit* of consciousness he finds the "good ambiguity"[27] which he had previously defined as "a spontaneity which accomplishes what appeared to be impossible when we observed only the separate elements" ("I" 409/11); and that ambiguity, since it is a latent intentionality, is precisely, according to him, what characterizes *Erfahrung* as dialectical. In the very *Bewusstsein,* Merleau-Ponty sees the contours of a *fissure*[28] that has to be considered as "the locus of a single explosion which produces selfness and consciousness of something" (*NC* 302/37); in the order of the phenomenon—neither subject nor object, but their common "hidden frame" (*NC* 297/32)—he recognizes a "new ontological milieu, which is the *Erscheinung*" (*NC* 306/41 trans. modified) understood as the self-appearing in "watermark" (*NC* 319/52) of the absolute. Therefore, in this very dialectical movement of the self-appearing of the absolute, Merleau-Ponty recognizes "what makes the leaving of oneself be a retiring into oneself, and vice versa." That is what *The Visible and the Invisible* suggests "true philosophy" has "to apprehend." Briefly stated, it is a question of the principle that gives rise to the segregation of interior and exterior, as well as to their reversibility.

Concerning the problem of the "relationship between phenomenology and absolute knowledge (metaphysics)," Merleau-Ponty therefore comments: "the phenomenological theme (*erscheinende Wissen,* the blossoming of knowledge) seems to imply an overthrowing of philosophy. There is no absolute *An sich,* and no absolute *für uns,* for the same reasons, i.e., their reciprocal relativization, their 'mutual intertwining' [*Ineinander*]" (*NC* 304/39). The emerging of knowledge and—what is synonymous—the presence of the absolute to ourselves, show a conception according to which the absolute takes shape neither as a pure Object nor as a pure Knowledge, but as the Irrelative that dictates to the order of the phenomenon—where subject and object have not yet a distinct identity—segregation and reversibility.[29]

Thus, the absolute emerges as the "other side" (ibid.) of the *Erscheinung,* the order of the phenomenon, since it is its Irrelative, although, on the other hand, it needs that order, because, without it, it would not really be an absolute, but would remain—as Hegel writes—"lifeless and alone."[30]

It is in this sense that Merleau-Ponty previously observed: "an absolute knowledge does not prove itself to be absolute except in manifesting itself, in being born into phenomena" (*NC* 285/18–19); and more than once, in these notes, he echoes the judgment made by Hyppolite: "Phenomenology is the total part: the whole system under a certain relation" (*NC* 286/19).[31]

Thus, in his formulation of the theme of the phenomenology that seems to emerge from the thirteenth and fourteenth paragraphs of the "Introduction," Merleau-Ponty singles out an "overthrowing of philosophy," which suggests, as he notes, that this very "philosophy seems to have entered into the phenomena," namely to be converted into "a-philosophy." But he immediately adds: "But then there is para.15" (*NC* 301/36).[32]

Which Absolute Knowledge?

In the fifteenth paragraph of the "Introduction," Merleau-Ponty sees a radical modification in the consideration of experience and in the characterization—intimately tied to the former—of the philosophical attitude.

Previously, in fact, experience had appeared as "ambiguous"[33] as the consciousness with which it was at one, "discontinuous" (*NC* 308/43), "errant, skeptical" (*NC* 312/46); and this is precisely how it was assumed by the philosopher, whose task was, according to Hegel, "the pure act of seeing"[34] another "pure seeing": the one in which for Merleau-Ponty the appearing of knowledge in experience[35] consists, inasmuch as it is a spontaneous self-articulation without, therefore, any *Sinngebung*. Now, on the contrary, on the basis of that same configuration, experience is judged as "erroneous, and blind," and accordingly in need of "a *Zutat* of philosophy" (*NC* 308 n. a/308 n. 63) that could transform it in its truth. As we know, Hegel in fact specifies that the natural consciousness finds in an accidental and external way the true object that substitutes for the preceding one; consequently its experience, considered in this way, does not appear as the appearing of knowledge. Nevertheless, it appears so in the philosopher's perspective, who introduces there an "addendum" consisting of "*a reversal of consciousness.*"[36] Thanks to this reversal, the new object shows itself as connected to the previous one in a necessary movement. "In short," according to Merleau-Ponty, "experience [is] necessary, but not sufficient. Experience must be understood—which requires 'conversion,' or 'reversal'" (*NC* 312/46). Therefore, this reversal (*Umkehrung*) does not appear to be made spontaneously by consciousness thanks to its *zweideutige* structure, a *zweideutige* structure by virtue of which it echoes the rhythm of the segregation and reversibility of the absolute. In contrast to what Merleau-Ponty's commentary pointed out in the previous paragraphs of the "Introduction," this reversal represents precisely the contribution of the philosopher. Thus, the reversal is to be understood as conversion rather than as reversibility.

Merleau-Ponty observes that, in this way, the philosopher, instead of limiting himself to "the pure act of vision," *adds* to the plane of experience that of the truth of this experience:[37] something that he himself had established. It follows that the Hegelian conception of philosophy as "addendum" means, on the one hand, that "science is not life" (*NC* 306 n. b/308 n. 62) and that there is a separation between philosophy and non-philosophy, while on the other it ends up in the "most violent dogmatism," since the latter is masked precisely as recourse to the truth of experience: "The others no longer know what they think. The philosopher understands them better than they understand themselves" (*NC* 309/43).

At this point, obviously, Merleau-Ponty can present the "solution"[38] that the last paragraph of the "Introduction"[39] offers to the contradictions he noticed: the "addendum" of the philosopher does not contradict his "pure act of vision," but is at one with it: in fact, what the philosopher apprehends and consciousness ignores is only that the figures of this latter are the moments of the truth of the mind. But consciousness itself will arrive at this awareness. In this way, it will come to "indicate" absolute knowledge, namely the form in which the absolute, in its turn, recognizes itself as self and thus reaches the plane of the Hegelian logic, where it will be looked at as Idea.

Reading the relation between phenomenology and metaphysics (with which, as we know, the Hegelian logic coincides) that Hegel draws in the "Introduction" in the light of the fifteenth paragraph, Merleau-Ponty will point to a certain "circularity." In fact, if, as that paragraph affirms, the phenomenon is identical in absolute knowledge with the essence, inasmuch as it is the manifestation of the absolute, it must then be admitted that phenomenology really "encompasses everything" (*NC* 315/49), and that natural consciousness is the "inverse" (*NC* 316/49) of that science to which the former ascends without the external intervention of a philosophical *Sinngebung*. On the other hand, phenomenology "encompasses everything," as Hyppolite specified, only "under a certain point of view": namely, that of consciousness and its figures. This is the reason why phenomenology refers back to the remaining "system of the science" and in particular to the *Logic,* where that "everything" is presented from the point of view of purely thinkable Being.

Merleau-Ponty judges the circularity of this formulation as an ambiguity conscious but fragile,[40] and he recognizes the sign of the subsequent fading away of that circular equilibrium precisely in the fact that the pages of the *Phenomenology of Spirit* on which he is commenting were originally without a title, whereas later they will be designated by Hegel as "Einleitung." This would betray the reconsideration of the phenomenology of spirit, shifting it from "the presence of the absolute" to "a part of science"[41] (*NC* 316–17/49–50) that clearly requires an "Introduction."

According to Merleau-Ponty, the break of that fragile equilibrium will lead, in the succession of Hegel's works—from the *Logic* to the *Encyclopaedia*[42]—to the dogmatism, or better, to the "skeptic-dogmatism" that he had already noticed in the fifteenth paragraph of the future "Introduction": on the one hand, experience is blind and needs the reversal of the consciousness; on the other, it teaches a lesson that only the philosopher is able to apprehend. In the first case, experience is nothing and the concept everything; in the second, the concept becomes nothing and experience becomes everything; but in both cases, the two terms separate: the absolute—which, as we saw, Merleau-Ponty interpreted as their *Ineinander*—becomes empty, reduced to a "mix of indifference and conservatism" (*NC* 320/53), while philosophy, in turn, leaving the ground of non-philosophy, becomes once again a "*Denken* of the overview" (*NC* 340/72).

Why this result? Because, according to Merleau-Ponty, even if Hegel had glimpsed the "Third term"[43]—namely the absolute as *Ineinander,* experience as the mutual "openness" between interior and exterior which precedes the dualism of subject and object, or, in a word, as the order of the phenomena preliminary to that dualism, and thus as a new ontological milieu—he never really distances himself from this very dualism, but remains subordinate to "a philosophy of consciousness, of representation and of the 'subject'" (*NC* 317/50). This shows itself precisely in the submission of experience to the philosophical *Sinngebung,*[44] which restores the distinction between the relation to the self and the relation to the exterior: a distinction which supports the claim that the *Denken* contains both, bringing the second back to the first.[45] According to Merleau-Ponty, then, it is precisely due to that subordination that the Hegelian description of the relations between interior and exterior slips inevitably into an equivocation, an ambiguity—we could affirm[46]—

which he once defined as "bad" ("I" 409/11) because, instead of seeking to reveal the "Third term," it only teaches the mix between the first two. In the final analysis, therefore, the phenomenology is reappraised and ontology (for Hegel this means logic) is once more superimposed on it, instead of being sought out *within* it. Here is, finally, the temptation to fabricate, "in the name of 'knowledge,'" "an illusory all-powerfulness—a negativity that is so total that it founds and digests everything and nothing" (*NC* 341/73). In other words, Merleau-Ponty assumes that Hegel affirms an absolute knowledge which "is presumed to have totalized, included *everything*, surpassed *everything*" (*NC* 317/50).

Merleau-Ponty certainly cannot share this conception of absolute knowledge, which represents just another variation of that "*Denken* of the overview" which, in different versions, constitutes the first target of the critical arguments in *The Visible and the Invisible.* Actually, that way of thinking ignores "the blind spot" of "the mind's eye,"[47] which, due to our relation of carnal involvement in the world, prevents us from any "exhaustiveness,"[48] because that relation extends, under the sign of reversibility, into the realm of thought.[49] Nevertheless, in the discussion above, we saw emerging some traces of an affinity between the conception of philosophy based on the idea of "hyper-reflection" that Merleau-Ponty planned to elaborate in *The Visible and the Invisible* and the conception of absolute knowledge he thinks he finds in some paragraphs of the "Introduction" to the *Phenomenology of Spirit.* The more explicit characterization he gives of this different configuration of absolute knowledge seems to be the one committed to a note written in the margins, where the twelfth paragraph of the "Introduction" ends:[50] "a knowledge in which subject and object, savage consciousness and reflected consciousness reciprocate each other. Both fall within knowledge, which is therefore not our *Sinngebung,* but the unfolding of the *Sache* as it is in and for-itself" (*NC* 300 n. a/306 n. 54).[51]

Here Merleau-Ponty shows precisely that he does not conceive absolute knowledge as a panoramic "point" (the term Hegel employs in the "Introduction"),[52] as a point that—like the one that reflective philosophy would occupy—could offer, retrospectively unfolded in reflection, the entire landscape of unreflected life. On the contrary, Merleau-Ponty conceives absolute knowledge—in analogy with what we noticed about hyper-reflection—as an awareness of the reversibility that is at work between reflection and the unreflected. And it is in this reversibility that the unfolding of the thing itself happens.

In this sense, Merleau-Ponty reaffirms the way that the ambiguous character of the truth[53] refers to the very ambiguity of consciousness, since it consists precisely in the co-originality and reversibility of savage consciousness and reflected consciousness, which alternate in the roles of that which is measured and that which provides the standard of measurement. This statement, in turn, shows that, conceived in this way, the "absolute knowledge in a sense precedes itself, since the measured is also the standard of measurement" (*NC* 300/34). In fact, since the absolute is always close to us, our "savage consciousness," as *Urdoxa,* has from the beginning a global knowledge of the absolute itself as its "natal place," so that every successive exploration of it finds something that, in a way, was already known.

This kind of absolute knowledge again takes shape, therefore, as a totalization, but in such a way that we could characterize it as "anticipation," and thus set it against totalization conceived as retrospective exhaustiveness. Just this is what the following passage in *The Visible and the Invisible* suggests: "The movement toward adequation . . . is not the returning to itself of an adequate Thought that would have inexplicably lost sight of itself . . . It is the prepossession of a totality which is there before one knows how and why" (*VI* 65/42). It follows, then, that philosophy, instead of being, as it seemed before, a retrospective truth added on to experience, now shows itself as an experience that apprehends *itself* questioning its own initial truth.[54] Thus, a working note of *The Visible and the Invisible* synthesizes that "Philosophy is the study of the *Vorhabe* of Being, a *Vorhabe* that is not *cognition* [*connaissance*], to be sure, that is wanting with regard to cognition [*connaissance*], to operation, but that envelops them as Being envelops the beings" (*VI* 257/204).

Although the *Vorhabe* of Being is not "cognition," nevertheless knowledge[55] takes shape as an "ascent" that happens "on the spot" itself of the *Vorhabe* of Being, and always refers to it and always takes nourishment from it, since its manifestation, as the visible is always of the invisible. As we know, what Merleau-Ponty names "knowledge properly so called" ("I" 405/7) is not for him a parameter external to the knowledge offered from experience. On the contrary, he holds that it is precisely in the sentence concluding the twelfth paragraph of the "Introduction" that the idea that "both are the same" is expressed. "The same" has to be understood, and "Third term" as well, as a name for the designation of Being as a unity which differentiates itself and guarantees reversibility between what is differentiated; it is "the same," as some working notes in *The Visible and the Invisible* record, as that which segregates itself in the body into the sensible and the sentient,[56] offering in this way the model for every reflection,[57] as well as a new definition of identity as a "difference of difference" (*VI* 318/264).[58] Thus, "the same" is also that whose dehiscence prolongs itself, as diacriticity of language, in the field of meanings considered "pure."[59] Moreover, "the same" is that which, since it dictates the reversibility that takes place between natural consciousness and science, makes knowledge possible precisely as an "ascent on the spot," without needing any "addendum" or any external reference. "The same" is therefore that which reveals the "identity by principle" (*VI* 325/272) of philosophy and non-philosophy. "The same," finally, is that which makes phenomenology and ontology *one within the other* (*Ineinander*).

What Language for Philosophy?

But let us return to Merleau-Ponty's idea of philosophy, which, in a negative way, emerges from his critical commentary on Hegel. According to that idea, philosophy must never cease "reconsidering itself, thinking itself as encompassed by an englobing: the present, vertical world" (NC 317/50), keeping in touch with the *Zweideutigkeit* which characterizes that world. Nevertheless, as the philosopher says a few pages later, "the very formulation of this living 'ambiguity' [*Zweideutigkeit*] makes experience disappear" (*NC* 319–20/53). This remark, which insistently recurs in the final part of his commentary notes to the "Introduction,"[60] does not appear here for the first time in Merleau-Ponty's works. We can also find it in *The Visible and the Invisible,* especially in the pages dedicated to the "bad" and "good" dialectic,[61] so classified, among other things, precisely because the former accepts and the latter refuses any formulation. But in some of those pages, Merleau-Ponty tends, without any explanation, to conflate the fact that dialectic cannot be formulated as such and the fact that it cannot be formulated into theses.[62] Therefore, in these preparatory notes we can see in a clearer way than in *The Visible and the Invisible* that Merleau-Ponty affirms that philosophy must not become fixed in formulas, that it must be self-critical, that it must not reduce itself to "spoken language" and must remain an "operative language" (*VI* 168/126). But he also wants to point out something deeper: that the philosophical formulation tends radically to betray the polymorphism of mute Being, going quite beyond the different mode of "stylization" necessarily imposed by the passage from perceptual to linguistic expression.[63] In fact, with regard to the famous Hegelian characterization of the absolute as "identity of identity and non-identity," these preparatory notes, noticing how the difference that results from this is a "subordinated" difference, point out that "this is inevitable as soon as [the difference] ceases being experience and becomes *signification,* something spoken (oldness)" (*NC* 317/50). And a little further on, these very notes continue: "I have said that the movement of experience to things spoken is inevitable. But this means that in a sense philosophy negates itself in formulating itself" (ibid.). But then the notes correct themselves: it will be inevitable, he now argues, if one remains in the field of "a philosophy of consciousness, of representation and of the 'subject'" (ibid.).

For philosophy, therefore, going outside this field would amount to articulating itself in a language no longer belonging to the horizon of consciousness, to the distinction between subject and object: the only language that could avoid denaturing the reversibility, "the passivity of our activity." But of this—not by chance—"philosophy has never spoken" (*VI* 274/221), even if it is the "dispossession" that it has to "grasp."[64] But how is such a philosophical language to take shape? If "the idea of *chiasm*" implies that "every relation with being is *simultaneously* a taking and a being taken, the hold is held, it is *inscribed* and inscribed in the same Being that it takes hold of" (*VI* 319/266), could it be once again the language of the *concept?*

"It would be," as Merleau-Ponty explains in *The Visible and the Invisible,* "a language of which he [i.e., the philosopher] would not be the organizer, words he would not assemble, that would combine through him by virtue of a natural intertwining of their meaning, through the occult trading of the metaphor—where what counts is no longer the manifest meaning of each word and of each image, but the lateral relations, the kinships that are implicated in their transfers and their exchanges" (*VI* 167/125). But this and the other few indications given by the last Merleau- Pontian texts surely are not enough to answer these questions in a full and final way. Nevertheless, these indications, if taken together with those offered by the practice of writing that Merleau-Ponty exercised in those texts, suggest that he was pursuing a language in which the philosopher would be dispossessed by that "constituting consciousness" which is his "professional impostor" (*S* 227/180). Dispossessed, however, not in order to be delivered over to a total, and unlikely, passivity—"we are not effects" (*VI* 274/221), he remarks—but rather in order that the philosopher could recognize himself as crossed by the chiasm between activity and passivity, precisely there where the reflexivity of Being, which is the unfolding of the thing itself, takes shape. In other words, Merleau-Ponty's research seems to go toward a language that does not suppose it can reduce itself to the purely denotative modes of conceptuality,[65] but knows itself as inevitably charged with the connotative values symbolized by the metaphor: a language, therefore, that could force the traditional opposition between the former and the latter,[66] drawing meaning from their common roots, sunk in the sensible world of analogy,[67] in order to undertake the task *The Visible and the In-*

visible suggests to hyper- reflection, namely, giving itself up to that world in order to "make it say, finally, what in its silence *it means to say*" (*VI* 61/39). On the other hand, the affirmation of a reversibility between unreflective life and reflective life implies that philosophical expression, traditionally conceived as a progression from the dark polymorphism of the unreflective to the conceptual consciousness of the reflective, is always doubled by a regression from conceptual consciousness toward the dark unreflective. In brief, the light of reflective consciousness is not given without the shadow of savage consciousness, and it is precisely in their intertwining that Being shows through.[68]

Thus, the "conclusion" to which Merleau-Ponty comes in his commentary on the "Introduction" to the *Phenomenology of Spirit* does not offer many alternatives. Merleau-Ponty writes: "1. Either, if consciousness protects its rights, it falls back into abstract positivism or negativism, and it creates a disjunction at the level of phenomena . . . ; or 2. philosophy can be left unformulated; in any case philosophy is whatever succeeds in passing for a notion of consciousness" (*NC* 320/53, trans. modified). He indicates a similar alternative in *The Visible and the Invisible,* where he reminds us that although the outlines of the second option are not yet definite, the first one would condemn philosophy to miss the world of "non-philosophy"—precisely that world which, on the contrary, it is called upon to bring to expression.[69] In this sense, we could say, Merleau-Ponty arrives *ad limina philosophiae.* And these limits, in turn, refer back to the very beginnings of philosophy, because the idea of an "a-philosophy" which "scoffs at philosophy" is nothing other than that of a thought which could make sense of the reasons for the laughter of the maidservant from Thrace.[70]

3

Nature: Variations on the Theme

Nature and Ontology

The last courses that Merleau-Ponty held at the Collège de France focus on the "concept of Nature" on the one hand, and the "possibility of philosophy today" on the other. Merleau-Ponty brings together under the first heading both the courses of 1956–57 and the courses of 1957–58—of these courses, the latter, centered on "Animality, the Human Body, Transition to Culture," purport to be the "continuation" of the former. In 1959–60, Merleau-Ponty uses his last course to discuss the further issue of "Nature and Logos: The Human Body." As for Merleau-Ponty's reflections on "the possibility of philosophy today," one can trace these not only to the 1958–59 course, where that expression actually appears,[1] but also to other courses: two courses which Merleau-Ponty's unexpected death left unfinished—"Philosophy and Non-Philosophy Since Hegel," as we just saw, and "Cartesian Ontology and the Ontology of Today"—and the remaining course of 1959–60, entitled "Husserl at the Limits of Phenomenology."

What is the connection between these two foci of attention toward which Merleau-Ponty's last reflections converge? Undoubtedly, the connection lies within the problem of what he called "new ontology": the problem of its configuration and of its philosophical formulation.[2] Indeed, the preparatory notes for the last course dedicated to the "concept of Nature"—the goal of which is to define the "place of these studies in philosophy" (N 263/203)—speak of "the ontology of Nature as a way toward ontology—a way that we prefer because the evolution of the concept of Nature is a more convincing propaedeutic, since it more clearly shows the necessity of the ontological mutation" (*N* 265/204). Evidently, by retracing the path of what Merleau-Ponty had previously defined as the "philosophical history of the idea of Nature" (*N* 117/83), as well as by exploring, with the help of contemporary science, the "problems posed" (ibid.) by this very history, these courses are an effort to show, once again, that a particular relationship operates between humanity and Being. This relationship eludes the modern formula that confronts subject and object. According to Merleau-Ponty, our epoch has made this relationship more evident, but hasn't been able to give an explicit philosophical formulation for it. This is most specifically the theme of the lectures on "Cartesian Ontology and the Ontology of Today"[3]

We have already mentioned this, but it is still worth emphasizing: Merleau-Ponty's inquiry concerning Nature is not the kind of inquiry that, as a result of its ontological orientation, confronts the scientific standpoint with an attitude of denial. Just the opposite: it holds that such a confrontation with the scientific perspective cannot be avoided, and advocates an attitude of critical listening.

Clearly, one should not expect to find in science a fully elaborated ontology capable of taking the place of the modern ontology, according to which Nature is the absolute Object and in which the Subject is *Kosmotheorós* (an equally absolute spectator). As Merleau-Ponty contends, science as such "does not provide an ontology, not even under a negative form. It has only the power to divest pseudo-evidence of its pretension to be evidence" (*N* 145/106). Still, the formulation of ontological hypotheses, which is the task of philosophy, ought to be based on the outcomes of scientific inquiries too. In fact, Merleau-Ponty consistently emphasizes the way in which currents of twentieth-century scientific inquiry decisively converge. According to him, they converge in "emptying of evidence" the opposing causalistic and finalistic conceptions of Nature—which he considers "concepts of *artificialism*"—(*RC* 117/151) along with the idea of the separability of existence and essence[4] (which he holds to be equally artificial).

Melody and Species

Merleau-Ponty sees a contribution to this kind of "emptying of evidence" in Jakob von Uexküll's theories. These theories see biology as an autonomous science inspired by Goethe's conception of knowledge of Nature, and consequently as essentially anti-Darwinian;[5] on this basis, they see as the specific task of biology the study of the reciprocal action between the organism and its environment. Onto his examination of

Uexküll's theories, Merleau-Ponty grafts the ontological hypothesis that he attempts to elaborate. In so doing, he presents his own hypothesis in an especially enlightening way.

Merleau-Ponty emphasizes that the notion of animal environment (*Umwelt*) put forth by Uexküll—and which Merleau-Ponty explicates as "the milieu that the animal gets for itself" (*N* 226/172, trans. modified)—is a novel one, and not to be embedded in Kant's or Schelling's philosophical framework (despite the fact that, according to Merleau-Ponty, Uexküll's thought sometimes appears to be settling it there).[6] According to Merleau-Ponty, the novelty of this notion consists precisely in the way it avoids both causalism and finalism, as well as a platonistic setting that would conceive it as an "essence outside of time."[7] Merleau-Ponty connects this conception to Marcel Proust's characterization of melody, drawing on a metaphor according to which Uexküll (with an explicit reference to the nineteenth-century embryologist Karl Ernst von Baer) states that "the unfurling of an *Umwelt* is a melody, a melody that is singing itself."[8]

On the basis of some pages from the first volume of the *Remembrance* to which we shall direct our attention later on,[9] Merleau-Ponty explains that Marcel Proust characterizes melody as a "Platonic idea that we cannot see separately" since "it is impossible to distinguish the means and the end, the essence and the existence in it" (*N* 228/174). He alludes to the fact that, for the main character of those pages of the *Remembrance,* a peculiar *idea* of love is incarnated in the sound of a melody—the melody of the *petite phrase* of Vinteuil's sonata—to such an extent that that idea of love becomes inseparable from Vinteuil's listening.

Merleau-Ponty builds on Uexküll's and Proust's conceptions, and sees in the different manifestations of zoological behavior the variations in which "the theme of the animal melody" (*N* 233/178)[10] finds its expression. More generally, he comes to interpret the crucial question of the relation between parts and whole[11]—be it the relation between the organs and the organism or between the organism and its territory, or for that matter the links between sexes, or those of individuals with one another and with their species—in terms of "a variable thematism that the animal does not seek to realize by the copy of a model, but that haunts its particular realizations" (ibid., trans. modified), prior therefore to both causalism and finalism.[12] Actually, as Uexküll nicely expressed by mentioning "a melody that is singing itself," it is even prior to the distinction between activity and passivity, a distinction in which, if we look thoroughly, even the preceding opposition between causalism and finalism finds its roots.

Echoing the concluding sentence of the essay "The Philosopher and His Shadow" (a true manifesto for the elaboration of the "new ontology"), we might say, therefore, that in the thematism mentioned above, Merleau-Ponty finds a sui generis teleology "which is written and thought about in parentheses."[13] In the summary of his first course on Nature, Merleau-Ponty underscores how this teleology, unlike the "proper" one, contributes to the characterization of Nature as "oriented and blind productivity."[14] The aspect of orientation here—as explained in the auditors' notes on Uexküll's framework—should be understood "as something similar to the orientation of our oneiric consciousness toward certain poles that are never seen for themselves, but which are, however, directly the cause of all the elements of a dream " (*N* 233/178).

Merleau-Ponty emphasizes that, on this basis, "we shouldn't see, in the very numerous individualities that life constitutes, corresponding separated absolutes, in relation to which every generality would only represent beings of reason" (*N* 247/189, trans. modified). He explains that, rather, they give "an ontological value back to the notion of species." (ibid.)[15] But what does he mean by the "ontological value" of the notion of species? And why does he deem this point so important that he returns to it again and again?[16] Finally, in what sense does returning an ontological value to the notion of species help to delineate the "new ontology" which Merleau-Ponty wants to work out?

Voyance

We might look for an answer to these questions in the preparatory notes of one of the two courses interrupted by Merleau-Ponty's death—a course which (unlike the other of the two) was scarcely documented until a few years ago. This course bears the title "Cartesian Ontology and the Ontology of Today." The notes for this course discuss how the experiences that are practiced in contemporary art and literature converge toward delineating a "new ontology," and how they serve to specify the features of this new ontology. From these notes emerge the developing lines that Merleau-Ponty wanted to follow in reconsidering, according to this new ontological perspective, the relation between the sensible and the intelligible, that is, the relation between existence and essence. (We repeat that Merleau-Ponty considered these developing lines to be *operating*—even if they are not made philosophically explicit—in contemporary ontology.) The notes are particularly clear in this regard.

At the very center of these developing lines is a notion—thematized at last—which had often, but only implicitly, been present in the later texts of Merleau-Ponty (it is formulated only once in *Eye and*

Mind).[17] This notion is *central* in reconsidering the relation between the sensible and the intelligible. It is the notion designated by the term *voyance.*[18]

Voyance literally means "clairvoyance," the "gift of double sight," but, in view of the misunderstandings that might occur if such a notion is given a platonistic interpretation, we shall continue to use the original French term. In an effort to fully understand the import of this notion, we shall turn to it after briefly reviewing the overall project for the course in which the notion appears.

As we have already suggested, the task of this course is to try (in part through a direct contrast with Cartesian ontology) to give a philosophical formulation to contemporary ontology, which—according to Merleau-Ponty—has until now found its expression particularly in art and in literature. The first stop that he envisions for his journey is thus a survey of the landscape of "contemporary ontology," as it has spontaneously and implicitly been delineated in art and in literature. "Especially in literature" (*NC* 391), he emphasizes at a certain point. This is worth noting for those who claim that the last phase of Merleau-Ponty's thought refers exclusively to painting. Merleau-Ponty's discussion of the *artistic* domain does indeed concentrate on painting, following the path already traced out in *Eye and Mind.* But when it comes to the recognition of the literary domain, here Merleau-Ponty intends to examine the work of Proust as well as the investigations of Valéry, Claudel, and other authors of the "recent literature" (*NC* 191) individuated in Saint-John Perse and in Claude Simon.[19]

Although unmentioned in this program, there is another literary reference that assumes a theoretically central position in the definition of the contemporary ontological landscape in Merleau-Ponty's view. This reference is Arthur Rimbaud's "Lettre du voyant." Merleau-Ponty arrives at this reference via a statement by Max Ernst that assimilates the present task of the painter to precisely the task that Rimbaud's manifesto assigns to the poet: "Just as the role of the poet since [Rimbaud's] famous 'Lettre du voyant' consists in writing under the dictation of what is being thought, of what articulates itself in him, the painter's role is to circumscribe and project what is making itself seen within himself."[20] Both have to bring to expression, as it were—in terms that inevitably recall Uexküll's notion of "a melody that is singing itself"—what following Merleau-Ponty we might call "the passivity of our activity" (*VI* 274/221), that is, the reflexivity of Being itself.

From this perspective, *voyance* ends up baptizing that "new bond between the writer and the visible" (*NC* 190) which Merleau-Ponty sees as enforced by the research he calls "modern" (though we were saying that it should be understood as contemporary) and which according to Merleau-Ponty can rediscover the "Renaissance beyond Descartes" (*NC* 175). As he explains, "[t]he moderns rediscover the Renaissance through the magical idea of visibility: it is the thing that makes itself seen (outside and inside), over there and here" (*NC* 390). While on the one hand Merleau-Ponty contends that "da Vinci vindicates *voyance* against poetry" (*NC* 183)—which, unlike painting, da Vinci considers to be "incapable of 'simultaneity'" (*NC* 175)—at the same time Merleau-Ponty notes that "moderns make of poetry also a *voyance*" (*NC* 183). Therefore, they show that poetry is indeed "capable of simultaneity." The frequent effort to bring simultaneity to expression is thus, according to Merleau-Ponty, one of the characteristic traits of contemporary ontology.[21]

At this point Merleau-Ponty departs from Descartes's view of vision. Descartes reduces vision to a kind of *thought*—a kind of thought that is stimulated by images, in just the way that thought is stimulated by signs and words. By contrast, Merleau-Ponty conjectures that the "unveiling of the '*voyance*' in modern art—a *voyance* which is not Cartesian thought—might have [an] analogue in the arts of *speech*" (*NC* 182–83, emphasis added). He suggests that "[p]erhaps, we should, instead of reducing vision to a reading of signs by thought, rediscover in speech, conversely, a transcendence of the same type that occurs in vision" (ibid.). Indeed, it is precisely to this that he thinks Rimbaud has contributed in a decisive way.

Voyance—which, in the mutual referring of perception and the imaginary, "renders present to us what is absent" (*OE* 41/132)—therefore characterizes seeing in Merleau-Ponty's conception. As Heidegger reminds us, seeing is not *vor-stellen,* that is, "to represent by frontal positioning" and, by doing so, "to subject."[22] Seeing should instead be regarded as "complying with"—a verb which expresses the indistinguishability of activity and passivity. With *voyance,* we discover that seeing is a complying with the showing of the sensible universe itself, within which we find ourselves and through which runs the power of analogy.[23] By virtue of this power, bodies and things recall each other, establish new relations, invent lines of force and of flight, and, in the end, draw what Husserl expressed as a "*logos* of the aesthetic world."[24] This expression of Husserl's is often used by Merleau-Ponty precisely because of the reconsideration it suggests of the relationship between the sensible and the intelligible.

As a result of the fact that it offers this characterization of seeing, *voyance* helps to characterize that "ontological mutation" which—in relation to the concept of Nature—we have seen promoted by Merleau-Ponty's effort: the "mutation of the relationship between humanity and

Being" (*OE* 63/139, trans. modified) that in *Eye and Mind* he confesses to feeling "when he holds up a universe of classical thought, contrasting it en bloc with the explorations of modern painting" (ibid.), the same mutation that a dense working note of *The Visible and the Invisible* finds manifest in "atonal music" (atonal music is in fact assimilated to "paintings without identifiable things, without the *skin* of things, but giving their *flesh*"),[25] that very mutation that, therefore, consists in a *carnal* configuration of the relationship between humanity and Being. This mutation is obviously not expressible in the language of consciousness, of representation, of the modern frontality between subject and object. This is why Merleau-Ponty judges contemporary literature as linking, with the visible, that "new bond" which might be configurable as *voyance.*

After having examined the conception of language that Descartes expressed with regard to the idea of a universal language,[26] and after having seen in this conception "the equivalent of the theory of perspective" (*NC* 183),[27] Merleau-Ponty turns to the contrasting contemporary conception of language, which—according to him—characterizes language "not as an instrument in which thought would be as the pilot in his boat—but as some sort of substantial union of thought and language—Language not governed, but endowed with its own efficacy" (*NC* 186). The "Lettre du voyant" becomes an emblem of this contemporary conception, since there the autonomy of language is pushed to such a point that poetry is supposed to be *voyance.* This is why Merleau-Ponty considers Rimbaud "a fundamental milestone within a development of literature which began before and continues after him" (*NC* 187). Echoing that "mutation of the relationship between humanity and Being" that *Eye and Mind* sees expressed by painting, Merleau-Ponty writes: "It might be the case of a change of the relationship with the Being in the writer starting from Romanticism" (*NC* 187). As we have already seen, the change he has in mind is a change of the relationship between the visibility of the first and the speech of the other, which—instead of aiming at designating meanings[28]—mixes with things and, just as, for Rimbaud, "the wood which finds itself a violin," becomes a sensible emblem of the sensible itself.[29]

Merleau-Ponty sees another manifestation of this change (while claiming that this very manifestation entails a sketch of a non-platonistic theory of ideas)[30] in the pages of the first volume of the *Remembrance,* pages to which he returns again and again throughout the course of his reflections and to which we have already seen him connect Uexküll's melody metaphor. These pages are those in which Proust distinguishes "musical ideas"—as well as literary ones, and also "our notions of light, of sound, of perspective, of physical pleasure, the rich possessions wherewith our inner temple is diversified and adorned"—from the "ideas of the intelligence." The former are "veiled in shadows" and therefore "impenetrable to the human mind, but none the less perfectly distinct from one another, unequal among themselves in value and significance."[31]

Thus, the preparatory notes we are considering have an additional point of interest, insofar as, by newly examining just those pages of the *Remembrance* that *The Visible and the Invisible* was commenting on when it was interrupted by its author's sudden death,[32] they suggest what the developments of that commentary might have been.

The Visible and the Invisible defines as "sensibles" the ideas described by Proust,[33] for they appear to be inseparable from their sensible presentation (as we have seen even when Merleau-Ponty connects them to Uexküll's melody metaphor). It is to our sensible finitude, therefore, that they are offered.

The course notes proceed to consider, in their own right, the grounds on which such ideas had been assimilated by Proust to the notion of light in particular. In fact, as Merleau-Ponty explains, the encounter with these ideas, just like the one with light—"visible light" (*NC* 194), he specifies—and just like the one with the sensible, is an "initiation to a *world,* to a small eternity, to a dimension which is by now inalienable—Universality through singularity" (*NC* 196).

Moreover, the notes continue, "here just as there, in light just as in the musical idea, we have an idea which is not *what* we see, but is behind it" (ibid.). If, on the one hand, this transcendence restrains us from possessing such ideas—from conceptually grasping them, as light is likewise ungraspable—on the other hand, it compels them to show themselves (again just as light does) in what they illuminate. Something similar happens to the idea of love in the *petite phrase* of Vinteuil's sonata that had once been the "national anthem" of Swann and Odette's love.

Therefore, it is toward such transcendence that the sensible finitude is an opening: that very "transcendence of the same type that occurs in vision," which, as we have seen, Merleau-Ponty holds that we should rediscover in speech and which he recognizes in Rimbaud's poetics of *voyance.* It is, precisely, the transcendence of *voyance:* not "second sight" directed to the intelligible, but rather a vision that sees the invisible in the visible and thus allows us to find, within the very veil of music or of literary speech, the invisible of the idea that shines through—as Proust has taught us.

"Generality of Things"

We find here an explanation for why Merleau-Ponty insists on the importance of returning an ontological value to the notion of species.

More generally, the notion of *voyance* has the merit of making clear the sense of the question—at first glance a surprising one—that appears in a working note of *The Visible and the Invisible* dated November 1959: "Generality of things: why are there several samples of each thing?" (*VI* 273/220, trans. modified). Judging by what we have said up to now, the sentence that immediately precedes this question seems to give it an answer: "the things are Essences at the level of Nature" (ibid.).

In other words, each thing as generality is a sensible idea. Likewise with each species.[34] Returning an ontological value to the notion of species, therefore, means to recognize this notion as a sensible idea, rather than to consider it merely as a "being of reason." It certainly isn't an idea in the platonistic sense, which—as Merleau-Ponty emphasized—would remain "outside of time" as well as outside of space: an idea that would be presupposed as an *originary* by its samples. On the other hand, neither is it an empiricist inductive generalization,[35] which inevitably would take place a posteriori with respect to the samples. Rather, as we have seen, it is a generality that, as a "transtemporal and transspatial element" (N 230/176), shines through ("*trans*") its samples. In fact, these samples are what provide us with the *initiation,* "that is"—as Merleau-Ponty explains in *The Visible and the Invisible,* commenting on Proust's thought—"not the positing of a content, but the opening of a dimension that can never again be closed, the establishment of a level in terms of which every other experience will henceforth be situated. The idea is this level, this dimension. It is therefore . . . the invisible *of* this world, . . . the Being of this being" (*VI* 198/151).

The sensible idea is, therefore, a "dimension" which opens up simultaneously with our encounter with its samples, thus offering to us an anticipation of knowledge which "can never again be closed." The sensible idea thus turns out to be marked by a temporality—to which also the term "initiation"[36] refers—which is similar to the one that marks the rhythm of a melody. In discussing Uexküll's metaphor, in fact, Merleau-Ponty reminds us that "in a melody, a reciprocal influence between the first and the last note takes place, and we have to say that the first note is possible only because of the last, and vice versa" (*N* 228/174).[37]

In Merleau-Ponty's view, it is this very temporal structure that seems to allow Uexküll's notion of *Umwelt* to escape the opposing "concepts of *artificialism,*" that is, causalism and finalism. The notion of *Umwelt* does not claim to be outside of time, nor is it subjected to the law of temporal succession. Consequently, it avoids the separation between the sensible and the intelligible, existence and essence, variations and theme.[38] Thus, the (animal) theme only exists *together* with the variations that on the one hand deny it—being variations—but that by this very negation indirectly affirm it.

Hence, mediated by the description given by Proust of the musical idea, Uexküll's perspective seems to characterize the theme as the *absent,* which only its own variations can indirectly make present[39] and which is therefore *inseparable* from and *simultaneous* with them. The variations themselves constitute the theme, without, however, exhausting it: they constitute it as their own excess,[40] as it were. The connection traceable here between Uexküll's and Proust's conceptions takes us back to what Merleau-Ponty already reminded us in his first work: "in the melody each [note] is demanded by the context and contributes its part in expressing *something which is not contained in any one of them and which binds them together internally*" (*SC* 96/87, emphasis added).

It is in this light that the sensible idea itself, in relation to its own samples, finds its definition. The notion of *voyance,* which for Merleau-Ponty asserts its rhythm in simultaneity, allows us to rethink the relation between the sensible and the intelligible: in our vision, the particular, while offering itself as such, *contemporaneously* dimensionalizes itself and becomes a universal, like "a note that becomes tonality."[41] In other words, the particular becomes an "element" to which we are *initiated.* The *voyance* thus enables us to trace the genesis of the sensible idea—or, in other words, the sensible genesis of the idea—in the vision of the individualities *amongst* which the generality takes its shape, and—like "something which is not contained in any one of them and which binds them together internally"—it radiates throughout these very individualities, eliciting the glimmering of an anticipation of knowledge.[42]

The sensible idea, then, should not be conceived as an abstract substitute for what is perceived, as though it were its imprint and, as such, separable and therefore graspable. Rather, it should be understood—as we mentioned above—in terms of an *absence,* which is for this reason always *missed* in every attempt to grasp.[43] It is an absence indirectly presented by its samples.

The *voyance*—which, on the analysis that we have so far proposed, sees in a given entity the shaping of its own Being, and which therefore cannot separate existence and essence—comes to manifest itself as *Wesensschau.* However, it does not consist in the operation of a Subject that is *Kosmotheorós* in a modern sense, but rather in a thinking that is one with that sensible seeing that we have proposed to define as "*complying with,*" *from within,* the showing of the sensible itself. This is thus a thinking that works through a *carnal Wesensschau*[44] that, precisely for this reason, is a *synesthetic* one.[45] To use the brilliant expression appearing as the title of Paul Claudel's book (to which Merleau-Ponty himself refers in his lectures on "the ontology of today"),[46] we might say that this is the *Wesensschau* of a *listening eye:* an expression which, synesthetically, refuses any analytical separation between the sensory fields and more particularly between the presupposed activity of seeing and the presupposed passivity of listening. By conferring a mature philosophical formulation to the operation of this eye, we might perhaps reach the "new ontology" Merleau-Ponty hoped to elaborate.

4

The Thinking of the Sensible

The Problem of the Concept

In a working note to *The Visible and the Invisible,* Merleau-Ponty writes that philosophy "shows by words[, l]ike all literature," and he continues in the same note by saying that there is "no absolutely pure philosophical word" (*VI* 319/266).

The proximity of philosophy to literature in this note—a note moreover that attempts to "elaborate an idea of philosophy"—confirms what Merleau-Ponty claims in the last manuscript pages of *The Visible and the Invisible:*[1] the passage from the "ideality of the horizon" to "'pure' ideality," from "sensible ideas" to "ideas of the intelligence," that is, from the "conceptless" to the "conceptual," does not imply a liberation from visibility. Rather, the passage implies a *metamorphosis* of the flesh of the sensible into the flesh of language. This "metamorphosis"—a term that appears a couple of times in these last pages—does not cancel the horizonal structures of the sensible. Indeed, the endless becoming of sense is due to these horizons. Thus, horizonal structures persist even in the linguistic form that science considers as purified of horizons and therefore as "mature": the algorithm (*PM* 9/4).[2] The same final pages of *The Visible and the Invisible* give an important indication of the way in which Merleau-Ponty planned to develop his views on this subject. In these pages, Merleau-Ponty maintains that "the system of objective relations, the acquired ideas [i.e., those 'of the intelligence'], are themselves caught up in something like a second life and perception, which make the mathematician go straight to entities no one has yet *seen* [emphasis added], make the *operative* [Merleau-Ponty's emphasis] language and algorithm make use of a *second visibility* [emphasis added], and make ideas be the other side of language and calculus" (*VI* 201/153).

It is clear, therefore, that Merleau-Ponty qualifies the *sensible configuration* of the perceived thing as the "archetype" (*VI* 210/158) of what in our previous chapter we called a *carnal configuration,* which exists equally in the language of the idea, of the concept, and of the algorithm.[3] In this regard, Merleau-Ponty also asserts that language participates in ontogenesis;[4] language is *co-originating* with brute being. Note that this assertion does not mean that there is no "world of silence"—even if "non-language significations . . . are not . . . *positive*" (*VI* 225/171). Rather, the assertion that language is co-originating with brute being means that "the structure of [the] mute world is such that all possibilities of language are already given in it" (*VI* 203/155). In fact, language is not configured as a "second layer" which translates a primordial layer (which, in turn, would be conceived as a positive "original text"). Instead, language is conceived as the "metamorphosis" of the primordial layer, a metamorphosis that renews the carnal configuration of the mute world, but in "another flesh" (*VI* 200/153).[5] Like the sensible (which, nevertheless, always envelops language with its own silence), language itself is a "total part."[6] Like the sensible, it functions "by encroachment [*empiétement*]" (*VI* 271/218), and so—by virtue of its own being—it itself brings the Being to expression. Language also, therefore, exceeds itself; it says "as a whole more than it says word by word" (*PM* 182/131). In this way, a ray of Essence shines through its nets. In a passage from *The Visible and the Invisible* we have already seen in our previous chapter, Merleau-Ponty writes: "[t]he Essences are *Etwas* at the level of speech, as the things are Essences at the level of Nature" (*VI* 273/220).

Concerning this question, a working note in *The Visible and the Invisible* devoted to the *problem of the concept* notes that "[t]here is no longer a problem of the concept, generality, the idea, when one has understood that the sensible itself is *invisible,* that the *yellow* is capable of setting itself up as a level or a horizon" (*VI* 290/237).[7] In fact, if the sensible can, in its individual visibility, outline its invisible generality, if the yellow is able to offer itself as an individual and as an element at the same time, then this indicates not only that the sensible immediately gives itself *with* its invisible, but also that it immediately can give itself *as* an invisible, and not as its opposite.

What this comment means is that the concept is no longer a problem when it undergoes a "resignification" in the direction of the anti-Platonism that, according to Merleau-Ponty, Proust prefigures. As we know, in fact, Proust describes "ideas" which do not preexist independently of their sensible presentation.[8] Rather, they are inseparable from and simultaneous with their sensible presentation, since only the sensible presentation provides us with the "initiation" to them: ideas which are "there, behind the sounds or between them, behind the lights or between them, recognizable through their always special, always unique manner of entrenching themselves behind them" (*VI* 198/151). In a similar vein, in the working note we quoted above Merleau-Ponty insists that: "*every concept is first a horizonal generality, a generality of style*" (*VI* 290/237).[9]

It is precisely in this direction that Merleau-Ponty's thought seems to be moving when he takes up what he calls in "Everywhere and Nowhere"[10] "our"—epochal—"philosophical problem": "to open the concept without destroying it" (*S* 174/138). Note that Merleau-Ponty is concerned with "opening" not only the concept, but also all the other categories underlying Western thought, and that by "opening," he means rediscovering "the source from which they derive and to which they owe their long prosperity" (*S* 174/139). It is in this way that Merleau-Ponty tends, as we said above, to "resignify" the concept. On the one hand, he aims to reactivate the concept's motivations in order to conserve its "rigor" (*S* 174/138). On the other hand, he aims to abandon, as Proust's description of sensible ideas teaches,[11] the pretense to the "intellectual possession of the world" (*S* 174/138) that the concept seems always to exhibit.

Merleau-Ponty also criticizes this kind of pretense—and in exactly the same terms—in the working note we quoted at the beginning of this chapter. Here, in fact, on the basis of the very "idea of the *chiasm*" (that is, on the basis of the idea that "every relation with being is *simultaneously* a taking and a being taken"), Merleau-Ponty explains that philosophy "cannot be total and active grasp, *intellectual possession*" (*VI* 319/266, emphasis added). This implies what Merleau-Ponty maintained in "Indirect Language and the Voices of Silence," that is, that "[n]o language"—not even that of philosophy—"ever wholly frees itself from the precariousness of mute forms of expression, reabsorbs its own contingency, and wastes away to make the things themselves appear" (*S* 98/78).

How, then, does Merleau-Ponty envision this "showing by words" that, as we have seen, characterizes the proximity of philosophy to literature in his view? In order to clarify what *The Visible and the Invisible* calls, with a term that is consciously inadequate, the "object" of philosophy, Merleau-Ponty explains: "[t]he effective, present, ultimate and primary being, the thing itself, are [*sic*] in principle *apprehended in transparency* through their perspectives, offer themselves therefore only to someone who wishes not to *have* them but to *see* them, not to hold them as with forceps, or to immobilize them as under the objective of a microscope, but *to let them be* and to witness their continued being—to someone who therefore limits himself to giving them the hollow, the free space they ask for in return, the resonance they require" (*VI* 138/101, emphases added).

In this dense passage, the attitude of philosophy in relation to its "object" is discussed in terms of "seeing," which is understood, as we said in our previous chapter, as a *complying with.* Characterized in this way, the attitude of philosophy implies the renunciation of the claims to an intellectual possession of the *Begriff;* and becomes instead a "letting-be." This last expression—which is not the only one inspired by Heidegger—is repeated a few lines later to designate perception itself, where perception is significantly defined also as an "interrogative thought": "It is necessary to comprehend perception as this interrogative thought which lets the perceived world be rather than posits it, before which the things form and undo themselves in a sort of gliding, beneath the yes and the no" (*VI* 138/102).

Here Merleau-Ponty's approach seems to extend, to the entire sensible domain, Kant's characterization of the limited domain of the beautiful, at least according to the interpretation that Heidegger proposes, in his Nietzsche lectures, on the first moment of the judgment of taste.[12]

Letting-Be according to Heidegger and Merleau-Ponty

In Heidegger's opinion, Schopenhauer "misinterprets" the first moment of the judgment of taste given by Kant in *The Critique of Judgment:* the beautiful as the object of a disinterested delight. Schopenhauer interprets the *absence of all interest* as the more common notion of "*indifference* toward a thing or person."[13] Consequently, he claims that the aesthetic state occurs when "the will is put out of commission and all striving brought to a standstill."[14] Instead, Heidegger explains that "to take an interest in something suggests wanting *to have it for oneself as a possession, to have disposition and control over it.* . . . Whatever we take an interest in is always already *taken,* i.e., *represented,* with a view to something else."[15] Heidegger's own interpretation is that, for Kant, the process by which we find something beautiful "never can and never may" have an interest as its determining ground. "That is to say, in order to find something beautiful, we must *let* what encounters us, purely as it is in itself, come before us in its own stature and worth."[16] Thus, the behavior that Kant initially defined negatively as devoid of interest—the "comportment toward the beautiful"—manifests itself, according to Heidegger, as "*unconstrained favoring* [*freie Gunst*]." (In the fifth paragraph of the *Cri-*

tique of Judgment, Kant in fact characterizes the disinterested delight toward the beautiful by that very expression.) Heidegger comments as follows: "we must *freely grant* to what encounters us as such its way to be; we must *allow* and bestow upon it what belongs to it and what it brings to us."[17]

While in Schopenhauer's misinterpretation, the "unconstrained favoring" would mean indifference and suspension of will, thereby preventing every "essential relation to the object,"[18] in contrast, Heidegger maintains that this very behavior—"*letting the beautiful be what it is*"[19]—would favor the essential relation to the object and would therefore be the first "magnificent discovery and approbation" of aesthetic behavior.[20] In fact, aesthetic behavior would be freed from the metaphysical stamp to which it has always been traditionally subject: "for the first time the object comes to the fore as pure object and . . . such coming forward into appearance is the beautiful. The word 'beautiful' means *appearing* in the radiance of such coming to the fore."[21]

Disinterestedness characterizes, therefore, the real *openness*[22] of the subject to the world. The subject frees himself or herself from every interest, simultaneously liberating the object of the aesthetic contemplation, or, to quote Heidegger again, "letting the beautiful be what it is," *leaving it free* to *appear* as it is. Heidegger, then, asks: "is not such unconstrained favoring rather the *supreme effort* of our essential nature, the *liberation* of our selves for the *release* of what has proper worth in itself, only in order that we may have it purely?"[23] The disinterestedness that, according to Kant, characterizes the delight toward the beautiful is, according to Heidegger, deeply connected to "letting the being be" in its disclosure, and—Heidegger believes—this "letting-be," in turn, defines freedom as the condition of truth understood as unconcealment.[24] Moreover, "letting-be" has an essential connection not only with what Heidegger claims to be the meaning the term λόγος inherits from the verb λέγειν—"letting be seen" or "letting-appear" (*erscheinen lassen*)[25]—but also with thinking understood as *Gelassenheit* ("releasement" or "calmness").

In *The Life of the Mind,* Arendt offers the following precious and synthetic recapitulation of this line of thinking: "[t]he mood pervading the letting-be of thought is the opposite of the mood of purposiveness in willing; later, in his reinterpretation of the 'reversal,' Heidegger calls it 'Gelassenheit,' a calmness that corresponds to letting-be and that 'prepares us' for a 'thinking that is not a willing.' This thinking is 'beyond the distinction between activity and passivity.'"[26]

Nevertheless, in the most important of Heidegger's writings about *Gelassenheit*—the "Conversation on a Country Path about Thinking" written in 1944–45[27]—the letting-be of *Gelassenheit* that, according to Arendt, is intended by Heidegger as the opposite of purposiveness, seems to be viewed instead by Heidegger as a *purposiveness* to achieve *Gelassenheit.* We find here not a revocation of the will, but an echo of disinterestedness understood as "the supreme *effort* [*Anstrengung*] of our essential nature"—with its inevitable ethical resonances—that we already encountered in the Nietzsche lectures. Thus, in the "conversation," significantly entitled *Zur Erörterung der Gelassenheit,* Heidegger—confirming yet again the limits of his consideration of the sensible—indicates that *Gelassenheit* resides in the linguistic-ontological "place" (*Ort*) called "the Open" (*das Offene*), the place in which, according to his most famous discussions, beings manifest themselves in the truth of their relationship with Being. If Arendt is right, then by virtue of this "placement," *Gelassenheit* lies "beyond the distinction between activity and passivity," but it seems to us on the basis of Heidegger's remarks here that instead *Gelassenheit* maintains the *oscillation* between activity and passivity. Indeed, the very definition of the essence of *Gelassenheit* as "this restless to and fro between yes and no"[28] implies oscillation.

Earlier, we asserted that Merleau-Ponty extends to the entire domain of the *aisthesis* the "approbation" of the aesthetics whose sources Heidegger locates in Kant's doctrine of the beautiful. This extension seems to be the meaning of the "ontological rehabilitation of the sensible" discussed in "The Philosopher and His Shadow." We must emphasize, then, that Merleau-Ponty—unlike Heidegger—puts letting-be in a place that lies "beneath the yes and the no,"[29] that is, in what we will see Merleau-Ponty calling "the initial yes, the undividedness of feeling" (*RC* 179/198–99).[30] It is the aesthesiological-ontological place where original intentionality ignites. Here we can see, therefore, the outlines of a thinking that does not operate "beyond," but *beneath* the distinction between activity and passivity. It is, in other words, a "logos of the aesthetic world," in which this genitive must be understood both in the subjective and in the objective sense, or rather as *neither* subjective *nor* objective. In fact, this logos sprouts beneath the subject-object distinction, revealing itself as a thinking of the sensible[31]—a thinking that is not a kind of reflection on Being from the outside, but rather itself a phenomenon, a manifestation of this Being.

As we saw, Heidegger's approach defines our disinterested openness to the world as "the supreme effort of our essential nature." It is therefore not really able—in our opinion—to evade the distinction between activity and passivity. According to Merleau-Ponty, that openness is instead initiated by virtue of what Henri Maldiney calls the "*événement-avènement*" of appearing.[32] Maldiney's "event-advent" is located beneath that distinction, or in any case leads back beneath it. In fact, the "event-advent" of appearing functions as an *aesthetic shock,* which ignites the astonishment in our encounter with the sensible, suspends our habits, and dispossesses us of the ability to distinguish reciprocally between the active and passive poles. Thus, echoing our last quote from *The Visible and the Invisible,* the interpretation of the unconscious given by Merleau-Ponty in the conclusion of his last course summary seems to move in this direction: "The unconscious is feeling itself, since feeling is not the intellectual possession of 'what' is felt, but a dispossession of ourselves in favor of it, an opening toward that which we do not have to think in order that we may recognize it. . . . the primordial unconsciousness would be the letting-be [*le laisser-être*], the initial yes, the undividedness of feeling" (*RC* 179/198–99, trans. modified).[33]

The Philosophy of a Baroque World

Let's return, now, to the characterization of philosophy as a "showing by words." In light of what has been said and of what we read in the passage from *The Visible and the Invisible* concerning the "object" of philosophy, the seeing implied there[34] has to be understood, in our opinion, as "apprehending in transparency" the thinking of the sensible—the logos of the aesthetic world—*letting it be* and thus giving back to it—in a never-ending phenomenological reduction[35]—"the resonance it requires." As "showing by words," language is indeed the resonance of the silence in which the sensible dwells, and upon which language itself feeds. Thus, language cannot claim to observe from the outside, it cannot claim not to be implicated, because, according to Merleau-Ponty, not even philosophical language "reabsorbs its own contingency, and wastes away to make the things themselves appear." Rather, Merleau-Ponty assigns to philosophical language the duty "to accompany" (*VI* 165/124) the breakup of the originating. Therefore, we have to understand philosophy's "showing by words" in the sense which we have already mentioned, the sense of "complying with"—through the creating of those words—the showing of the sensible *logos.*[36] This implies, in turn, our *taking part* in this showing, our complying with it *from within,* and then our pointing out our own *en-être* ("being of it"), "the passivity of our activity" (*VI* 274/221) of creation, according to what Merleau-Ponty defines as "hyper-reflection" (*VI* 61/38).[37] Even what Merleau-Ponty says about painting in *Eye and Mind*—where he emphasizes its *absence of interest*[38]—and what Merleau-Ponty says about the *voyance* of contemporary literature in the lectures on "Cartesian Ontology and the Ontology of Today"[39] imply this "taking part."

We saw that, precisely in these writings, Merleau-Ponty judges that contemporary art and literature—before philosophy and more effectively than philosophy—have succeeded in expressing the "mutation" in the relations "between humanity and Being" that he finds in our epoch. In other words, Merleau-Ponty seems to mean that contemporary art and literature—before philosophy and more effectively than philosophy—have begun from within to *comply with* the showing of the sensible, *letting be* its peculiar "logic of implication or promiscuity" (*RC* 71/118). Complying with this logic in which "every relation with being is *simultaneously* a taking and a being taken" (*VI* 319/266),[40] contemporary art and literature do not superimpose upon the sensible the antithetical logic of representation which for the most part has dominated philosophy.

The logic of seeing conceived as "representing by frontal positioning" is precisely what underlies the notion of concept according to which the subject *grasps* in thought the universal representation of the object positioned in front of it. In the last page of "The Philosopher and His Shadow," Merleau-Ponty provides the emblem of this logic of representation: the (supposed) representative frontality found in Renaissance perspective.[41] By contrast, Merleau-Ponty assimilates the being of the sensible to a "baroque world."[42] In this world, Merleau-Ponty sees a "configurational meaning which is in no way indicated by its 'theoretical meaning'" (or, better, by its *kosmotheoretical* meaning), even if—as Merleau-Ponty emphasizes—it is precisely this "brute mind" that is going to be "asked to create culture anew" (*S* 228/181).

We must therefore "resignify" the concept (to use our terms above) along the lines of the baroque configuration of the sensible—in which every taking is simultaneously a being taken and feeling is in reality a letting-be. In this way, we would renounce the claims of the *Begriff* to take "intellectual possession of the world" and we would enable conceptuality to speak, at last, about "the passivity of our activity." Perhaps this is exactly what Merleau-Ponty meant by his phrase, "to open the concept without destroying it." Certainly, such a "resignification" (which takes into consideration, as hyper-reflection teaches, the bond between conceptuality and conceptlessness, between conceptuality and the sensible as itself *invisible*—that is, the always *carnal* configuration of sense)[43] also implies the "resignification" of metaphoricity, which is traditionally opposed to conceptuality. Such a "resignification" of metaphoricity would lead us to recognize the deepest metaphorical origin of the concept.[44] Or better, it would lead us to recognize a common source of the concept and metaphor as "styles of being,"[45] which therefore plant their roots in the polymorphism of Being itself, in the "oneiric world of analogy" (*OE* 206/132), in short, in the excess of the sensible, not only in the excess of language.

Thus, it seems no accident that it is precisely in a discussion about a theorist of the baroque that we are reminded that the term "concept," in its Latin etymon, had a certain semantic halo whose traces one can discern in the "a-philosophical" thinking toward which Merleau-Ponty tends. In an essay on the Spanish baroque theorist Baltasar Gracián, we read: "Twentieth-century philosophy usually considers the term 'concept' as the translation of the German word 'Begriff.' This last word came to the attention of philosophical reflection because of the enrichment of a speculative complexity by German philosophers from Kant on. It happens, then, that we say 'concept,' but we think *Begriff:* what escapes us is that the word of Latin origin has an opposite semantic orientation to that of the German word."[46] Specifically, *conceptus* differs from *Begriff* in the following way: while the etymon of the latter, via the verb *greifen,* refers to grasping (the exact English equivalent of *greifen*), the etymon of the former refers to an entity that is concave, and that, being concave, can function as a basin. This feature of meaning underlies not only the use of the verb *concipio* when it means "to be pregnant," but also the use that indicates "receiving something into one's spirit, one's thought, one's sense." This latter use is the source of the Latin meaning of "concept" as "mental conception."

Concavity, or hollowness, is therefore a crucial feature of the basic meaning of *conceptus.* On the other hand, we know that Merleau-Ponty frequently uses, in his last reflections, the term "hollow" (*creux*).[47] Furthermore, in this chapter we have seen Merleau-Ponty employing that term precisely to characterize the relationship between thinking and Being. In this light, the connection between Merleau-Ponty's thought and the Latin *conceptus* becomes more evident. The meaning of *conceptus* evokes the gesture of "welcoming" rather than the gesture of "grasping." Rather than the attitude of "subjecting," it evokes the attitude of "complying with." According to the meaning of *conceptus,* "to conceive does not mean to take possession of anything, but rather to create space for something."[48] And the direction of Merleau-Ponty's thinking seems to be exactly along these lines.

Notes

Preface

1. See *N* 265/204. Precisely because this mutation is, according to Merleau-Ponty, under way in our epoch, throughout this book we qualify it and its cultural symptoms as "contemporary," even though some of these symptoms, like the ones concerning art, are often defined as "modern" by Merleau-Ponty himself.

2. As is well known, the notes that anonymous auditors took throughout the first two cycles of courses devoted to the "Concept of Nature" have been published together with the notes that the philosopher himself drafted in preparation for the third course: see *N*. Moreover, the preparatory notes of the three courses entitled "La Philosophie aujourd'hui" (1958–59), "Philosophie et non-philosophie depuis Hegel," and "L'Ontologie cartésienne et l'ontologie d'aujourd'hui" (both held in 1960–61) are now published in *NC*. Lastly, the preparatory notes of the course entitled "Husserl aux limites de la phénoménologie" (1959–60) are now published in *OG*.

3. See, for example, *NC* 149ff. and *NC* 388–89.

4. See chapter 3, note 30.

5. See *N* 228ff/173ff.

6. See *VI* 138/101–2.

7. See chapter 1, note 35.

8. By "passively created" we mean that ideas turn out to be created in an *operative* way, and on this subject we recall that in a working note of *The Visible and the Invisible* Merleau-Ponty characterizes the operative intentionality as "the intentionality within being" (*VI* 297–98/244).

9. See *VI* 318/265.

10. In this sense Merleau-Ponty's notion of "flesh" seems to answer, among other things, the doubts raised by Jean-Luc Nancy, who saw in this notion merely the trace of a "philosophy of one's own body" (J.-L. Nancy, *Corpus*, 2d ed. [Paris: Métailié, 2000], 66). See also the shorter (and very different) English version of this text, *Corpus*, trans. Claudette Sartiliot, in J.-L. Nancy, *The Birth to Presence* (Stanford: Stanford University Press, 1993), 194. On the same topic, we refer the reader to our "Flesh: Towards the History of a Misunderstanding," *Chiasmi International*, n.s., 4 (2002).

11. "Nature is an enigmatic object, an object that is not an object at all; it is not really set out in front of us. It is our soil [*sol*], not what is in front of us, facing us, but rather, that which carries us" (*N* 20/4).

Chapter 1

1. As for this passage from Proust, see *R* 1:6/6–7. (We have cited from the English translation of Proust, rather than from *Phenomenology of Perception*—Trans.).

Concerning the pages of the *Remembrance* cited here, Florival notes that Proust "reveals himself instinctively to be a phenomenologist *avant la lettre* in his way of describing to us the discovery of the lived body" (G. Florival, *Le Désir chez Proust: A la recherche du sens* [Louvain, Paris: Nauwelaerts, 1971], 28).

2. In this same first section of his essay "The Novel and Metaphysics," Merleau-Ponty emphasizes that "[s]ince the end of the 19th century . . . the ties between [philosophy and literature] have been getting closer and closer" (*SNS* 46/27) since their common task has become to describe the "invasion" of the metaphysical in man at a time when "there is no longer any human nature on which to rely" (*SNS* 49/28). It also follows that "[p]hilosophical expression assumes the same ambiguities as literary expression, if the world is such that it cannot be expressed except in 'stories' and, as it were, pointed out" (*SNS* 46/27). The reference to Proust we made above takes on its full meaning in this context: as a consequence of his attitude, which we could define, by means of an expression from Merleau-Ponty, as "metaphysical and disinterested attention," the Proustian description of lived time reveals the metaphysical import of the way in which man lives time.

3. We find the same verb "to secrete" in Proust to indicate an identical process: "all this length of Time had not only, without interruption, been lived, experienced, *secreted* by me" (*R* 3:1047/1106, emphasis added). This is but a small example of the fact that, starting with *Phenomenology of Perception* and becoming more and more evident as time goes by, Proust's writing itself constitutes a fundamental point of reference for Merleau-Ponty. On this subject, see also the beginning of A. Simon, "Proust et l'earchitecture' du visible," in *Merleau-Ponty et le littéraire,* ed. A. Simon and N. Castin (Paris: Presses de l'École normale supérieure, 1997), 106. "Maurice Merleau-Ponty, from *Phenomenology of Perception* to *The Visible and the Invisible,* was 'haunted'—in the Merleau-Pontian sense of creative innervation—by Proustian thought and writing such as they are found in *A la recherche du temps perdu.*" To define Proust as "his model," as did Lyotard, does not seem to us then as without foundation. (Cf. J.-F. Lyotard, "La Philosophie et la peinture à l'ère de leur expérimentation: Contribution à une idée de la postmodernité," *Rivista di estetica,* no. 9 [1981]: 10; "Philosophy and Painting in the Age of Their Experimentation: Contribution to an Idea of Postmodernity," trans. Maria Minich Brewer and Daniel Brewer, in *The Merleau-Ponty Aesthetics Reader,* ed. Galen Johnson [Evanston: Northwestern University Press, 1993], 330.)

4. The most immediate points of reference of Merleau-Ponty's analysis are indicated by the very epigraph of this chapter, Heidegger (*Sein und Zeit*) and Claudel (*Art poétique*). In other respects, his analysis also borrows much from Husserl's reflections on this theme, in particular those found in *Vorlesungen zur Phänomenologie des inneren Zeitbewusstsein,* originally published in *Jahrbuch für Philosophie und phänomenologische Forschung* 9 (1928). Today, this work is published in *Husserliana,* vol. 10, ed. R. Boehm (The Hague: Martinus Nijhoff, 1966); *On the Phenomenology of the Consciousness of Internal Time,* trans. John Brough (Dordrecht: Kluwer Academic Publishers, 1991).

On the conception of the relation between Husserl and Heidegger which underlies Merleau-Ponty's reflections at this stage of his thought, Spiegelberg reminds us that he "did not seem to feel that there were any basic differences between them. Thus in the *Phénoménologie de la perception* he presented Husserl's phenomenological reduction, to be sure in his own reinterpretation, as the indispensable foundation for Heidegger's conception of being-in-the-world, and implied that Heidegger's '*philosophie existentielle*' was a legitimate prolongation of Husserl's phenomenology. Besides, the climactic chapter on 'Temporality' in the *Phenomenology of Perception* is preceded by a motto from *Sein und Zeit* and leans heavily on Heidegger's text" (H. Spiegelberg, *The Phenomenological Movement,* 3rd rev. and enl. ed. [The Hague: Martinus Nijhoff, 1982], 538).

5. M. Heidegger, *Sein und Zeit,* quoted by Merleau-Ponty (*PP* 471/412).

6. On the notion of *Präsenzfeld* in Merleau-Ponty with respect to Husserl, see P. Burke, "Merleau-Ponty's Appropriation of Husserl's Notion of 'Präsenzfeld,'" in *Husserl in Contemporary Context,* ed. B.C. Hopkins (Dordrecht: Kluwer Academic Publishers, 1997), 37–58.

7. "Husserl introduced the notion of retention, and held that I still have the immediate past in hand, precisely for the purpose of conveying that I do not posit the past, or construct it from an *Abschattung* really distinct from it and by means of an express act; but that I reach it in its recent, yet already elapsed, thisness" (*PP* 477/417).

It is nonetheless necessary to note how the very considerations which Merleau-Ponty develops on the function of the body in remembering allow a glimpse of his tendency to accentuate, in comparison with Husserl's transcendental phenomenology, the corporeal tonality of temporal experience, which in other respects emerges clearly in the page of Proust which he cites on this occasion. Thus Merleau-Ponty emphasizes that protentions and retentions "do not run from a central *I,* but from my perceptual field itself" (*PP* 476/416). The difference existing between Merleau-Ponty's perspective and that of Husserl has also been noted by one of the last assistants of the German philosopher, Ludwig Landgrebe, who illustrates it in this fashion: "Husserl also speaks of sedimented and habitual knowledge, of the imprint of preceding experiences, in the light of which the perceived appears as this thing or that thing. But he considers this as a possession of the I. Merleau-Ponty, on the contrary, wants to call attention to the fact that it is not a possession of the I but a possession of the body, which has learned to move about in the world in a purposive manner and without the least reflection, and which consequently operates a synthesis of the present and the past, which belongs to it as an acquisition, a synthesis thanks to which we can speak of a perception" (L. Landgrebe, "Merleau-Pontys Auseinandersetzung mit Husserls Phänomenologie," in *Phänomenologie und Geschichte* [Gütersloh: Gütersloher Verlagshaus Gerd Mohn, 1968], 178). This difference in comparison with Husserl's orientation, which, however it may be, is not yet explicit at this stage of his meditation, will be thematized and developed by Merleau-Ponty in the last phase of his thought, on the basis of motifs of reflection that will be provided, once again, by Proust's *Remembrance.* He will then be led to critique Husserl's analysis of temporality, as well as the ontology that underlies it.

On the differences between Husserl and Proust with respect to the conception of memory, see the chapter entitled "L'Encadrement du souvenir (Husserl, Proust et Barthes)" in R. Bernet, *La Vie du sujet: Recherches sur l'interprétation de Husserl dans la phénoménologie* (Paris: Presses Universitaires de France, 1994), 243–65.

8. P. Ricoeur, *Temps et récit,* vol. 2, *La Configuration dans le récit de fiction* (Paris: Seuil, 1984), 203; *Time and Narrative,* vol. 2, trans. Kathleen McLaughlin and David Pellauer (Chicago: University of Chicago Press, 1985), 137. Ricoeur wishes in fact to avoid "the hasty interpretation according to which the fictive experience of time in Proust would consist in equating time regained with involuntary memory" (202/136).

9. It is in the name of this privilege attributed to the present, "because it is the zone in which being and consciousness coincide" (*PP* 485/424), that Merleau-Ponty critiques (cf. *PP* 489/427) the primacy of the future affirmed by Heidegger, who represents nonetheless, as we have said, one of the principal sources of inspiration for Merleau-Ponty's account of time.

10. Ricoeur, *Time and Narrative,* 210/141.

11. Florival, *Le Désir chez Proust,* 122.

12. Cf. M. Heidegger, *Sein und Zeit* (Tübingen: Max Niemeyer, 1953), §80, 419ff.; *Being and Time,* trans. Joan Stambaugh (Albany: State University of New York Press, 1996), 384ff. Originally published in *Jahrbuch für Philosophie und phänomenologische Forschung* 8 (1927).

Merleau-Ponty explains that "[s]ubjectivity is not in time, because it takes up or lives time, and merges with the cohesion of a life" (*PP* 483/422).

13. M. Merleau-Ponty, "Le Philosophe et son ombre," in *Edmund Husserl (1859–1959)* (The Hague: Martinus Nijhoff, 1959), 195–220, reprinted in *S* 201–28/159–81.

14. As Merleau-Ponty reminds us at the beginning of a working note citing the commentary of Lucien Herr on Hegel, "Nature is at the first day" (*VI* 320/267). He explains while commenting on this sentence in the summary of his first course on Nature: "It presents always as already there before us, and yet as new before our gaze. Reflexive thought is disoriented by this implication of the immemorial in the present, the appeal from the past to the most recent present. For reflexive thought each fragment of space exists on its own account and they can only coexist under its gaze and through its activity; each moment of the

world ceases to exist when it ceases to be present and is only held in past being by reflexive thought. If it were possible to abolish in thought all individual consciousness there would remain only a flash of instantaneous being, extinguished no sooner than it has appeared" (*RC* 94–95/133).

The reference to Herr is drawn from his article "Hegel," in *Grande Encyclopédie,* vol. 19, 99ff.; reprinted in *Choix d'écrits,* vol. 2 (Paris: Presses Universitaires de France, 1932), 109–46. See also *N* 76/49.

15. The citation is drawn from M. Merleau-Ponty, "De Mauss à Claude Lévi-Strauss," *Nouvelle Revue française* 82 (1959): 615–31; "From Mauss to Claude Lévi-Strauss," reprinted in *S* 143–57/114–25.

Already, in the course summary from the Collège de France in 1954–55 on "Institution in Personal and Public History," this form of temporality is illustrated in an important way by Merleau-Ponty's use of Proust's *Remembrance,* as well as the history of painting. "The analysis of love in Proust reveals this 'simultaneity,' this crystallization upon each other, of the past and of the future, of subject and 'object,' of the positive and the negative" (*RC* 62/109). In the same way, he continues, "[t]hus, rather than a *problem,* there is an 'interrogation' of painting, which lends a common sense to all its endeavors and binds them into a history" (*RC* 63/110–11).

As is well known, the phenomenon of simultaneity is affirmed moreover in the very phrase by which the *Remembrance* ends: men, writes Proust, "simultaneously, like giants plunged into the years, . . . touch epochs that are immensely far apart, separated by the slow accretion of many, many days" (*R* 3:1048/1107). Merleau-Ponty seems to be alluding to this phrase in *NC* 197.

16. Here is the complete passage to which we have just referred: "As the ethnologist in the face of societies called archaic . . . must describe a mythical time where certain events 'in the beginning' maintain a continued efficacity; so also social psychology, precisely if it wishes to really know our own societies, cannot exclude a priori the hypothesis of mythical time as a component of our personal and public history" (*VI* 43/24). This passage demonstrates in an implicit way that Merleau-Ponty, as a philosopher and in reference to Western ontology, intends to accomplish a task analogous to that which he sees carried out by the ethnologist and required of the social psychologist.

Regarding the evocation of a mythical time by Freudian psychoanalysis (to which the last phase of Merleau-Ponty's thought gives new attention, an attention that was not unfamiliar with the contemporary research of Lacan), the course summary from the Collège de France in 1954–55 on "The Problem of Passivity: Sleep, the Unconscious, Memory"—which must be kept in mind in its entirety with respect to the problems discussed in this section—already notes that the Freudian description of the oneiric consciousness shows that "our dreams are not circumscribed the moment we dream them, but import *en bloc* into our present whole fragments of our previous duration" (*RC* 70/118). On the subject of "mythical time" in its relation with Merleau-Ponty's intention to advance, during this phase, toward an "ontological psychoanalysis," we will find interesting considerations in P. Gambazzi, "Fenomenologia e psicoanalisi nell'ultimo Merleau-Ponty," *Aut Aut,* n.s., nos. 232–33 (July–October 1989): §5, as well as in chap. 4 of Gambazzi, *L'occhio e il suo inconscio* (Milan: Cortina, 1999), 39–44.

This mythical time, which thus also palpitates in the "personal and public history" of Western man, is nevertheless not only evoked for Merleau-Ponty in the works of Proust, of Freud, or in the innovations of contemporary painting. In his essay "From Mauss to Claude Lévi-Strauss," cited above, he remarks in fact that in linguistic time itself "synchronics, like legendary or mythical time, encroaches upon succession and diachronics" (*S* 154/122–23). It is equally necessary to remember that, as we have already indicated, *Phenomenology of Perception* affirmed that "there is more truth in mythical personifications of time than in the notion of time considered, in the scientific manner, as a variable of nature in itself, or, in the Kantian manner, as a form ideally separable from its matter" (*PP* 482/422).

17. Cf. *R* 1:922/983–84. As Anne Simon points out, "[o]ne can understand . . . why Proust is a constant reference of *The Visible and the Invisible,* where the Proustian discovery of a generalized ontological opening finds itself, deepened and thematized as such" (Simon, "Proust et l''architecture' du visible," 109).

18. The course summary of "Institution in Personal and Public History" rightly begins by explaining that "the concept of institution may help us to find a solution to certain difficulties in the philosophy of consciousness" (*RC* 59/107). This calling into question of the philosophy of consciousness is deepened precisely in the last phase of Merleau-Ponty's thought and nourishes its ontological developments.

19. "The structure of the visual field, with its near-bys, its far-offs, its horizon, is indispensable for there to be *transcendence,* the model of every transcendence" (*VI* 284/231). Or again: "the solution [to the problem of subjectivity] is to be sought in vision itself; memory will be understood only by means of it" (*VI* 248/194). And moreover, "[d]epth is *urstiftet* in what I see in clear vision as the retention is in the present" (*VI* 273/219). In short, as Kaufmann explains, "spatiotemporal distancing must borrow the language of vision, or rather, distancing depends in its formulation only on an approximative first language of which the expression of visibility constitutes its profound sense" (P. Kaufmann, "De la vision picturale au désir de peindre," *Critique* 20, no. 211 [1964]: 1061).

20. This remark is also found in C. Capalbo, "L'historicité chez Merleau-Ponty," *Revue philosophique de Louvain* 73 (1975): 515.

21. See *VI* 222/168.

22. In this sense, Duchêne remarks that "the last works [of Merleau-Ponty] *extend* to the visible, the sensible, space, and language, the affection of self by self, composed of immanence and transcendence, an idea which had already been discovered as early as the *Phenomenology of Perception* with regard to time. Like time, the visible, the sensible, and language have two faces and are object-subject, seen-seeing, sentient-sensible. Flesh is this structure generalized" (J. Duchêne, "La Structure de la phénoménalisation dans la *Phénoménologie de la perception* de Merleau-Ponty," *Revue de métaphysique et de morale* 83, no. 3 [1978]: 395

n. 151; "The Structure of Phenomenalization in the *Phenomenology of Perception* of Merleau-Ponty," trans. J. Donceel [with extensive revisions by the editor], in *Merleau-Ponty: Critical Essays*, ed. Henry Pietersma [Washington, D.C.: Center for Advanced Research in Phenomenology and University Press of America, 1989], 74 n. 151). It nonetheless remains the case that this "extension" is not without implying a deepening and a rectification regarding the conception of time itself.

23. Already in the course summary on "The Problem of Passivity: Sleep, the Unconscious, Memory," Merleau-Ponty wrote: "For man, to live is not simply to be constantly conferring meaning upon things but to continue a *vortex of experience which has been set up at our birth,* at the point of contact between the 'outside' and he who is called to live it" (*RC* 59/115, emphasis added). In fact, by virtue of the spatiotemporal *Urstiftung,* he explains in *The Visible and the Invisible,* "The things—here, there, now, then—are no longer in themselves, in their own place, in their own time; they exist only at the end of those rays of spatiality and of temporality emitted in the secrecy of my flesh. And their solidity is not that of a pure object which the mind soars over; I experience their solidity from within insofar as I am among them and insofar as they communicate through me as a sentient thing" (*VI* 153/114).

24. Cf. in particular *R* 2:755–58/783–85. On the other hand, as Bernet reminds us, "for the Husserlian theory of recollection, forgetting is only an accident" and it "does not at all threaten the *continuity* between the present and the past of consciousness" (Bernet, *La Vie du sujet,* 248).

25. It seems interesting to us to emphasize how the themes of time and (Proustian) narrative are linked here in this way with those of memory and forgetting, which Ricoeur has found necessary to treat recently, considering them precisely as "median levels between time and narrative" (P. Ricoeur, *La Mémoire, l'histoire, l'oubli* [Paris: Seuil, 2000], i).

26. The bases of this conception are laid in the above-cited course summary on "The Problem of Passivity," in which Merleau-Ponty tries to show how, by conceiving the field of presence founded by our perceptual opening to Being in gestaltist terms, the alternative between conceiving memory as conservation or as construction disappears: "then there would be no question of any alternative between conservation and construction; memory would not be the opposite of forgetfulness, and it might be seen that true memory is to be found at the intersection of the two, at the moment where memory forgotten and kept by forgetfulness returns. It might then be clear that forgetfulness and memory recalled are two modes of our oblique relation with a past that is present to us only through the determinate void that it leaves in us" (*RC* 72/119).

27. We also find the critique of Husserlian intentional analytics in Merleau-Ponty's intervention at the Sixth Bonneval Colloquium (October 1959) on the unconscious. The summary, written by Pontalis, of Merleau-Ponty's comments (who had died in the meantime), in fact affirms that "the solution [to the problem of the unconscious] is also not to be found in phenomenology, at least as long as it is conceived as an intentional analytics that would positively distinguish and describe a series of operations or acts of consciousness" (M. Merleau-Ponty, Intervention in the discussion on "Langage et inconscient," in

L'Inconscient (VIe Colloque de Bonneval), ed. H. Ey [Paris: Desclée de Brouwer, 1966], 143).

28. In the light of Husserl's examples of pre-theoretical constitution, Merleau-Ponty in fact wonders on this occasion: "[a]fter we have made this descent, are we still entitled to seek in an analytics of acts what upholds our own and the world's life without appeal?" (*S* 208/165).

29. "The figure-ground distinction," according to a working note from *The Visible and the Invisible,* "introduces a third term between the 'subject' and the 'object.' It is *that separation* (*écart*) first of all that is the perceptual *meaning*" (*VI* 250/197). Regarding the change in the conception of transcendence we can observe in Merleau-Ponty's last texts, one must recall that, starting with *Phenomenology of Perception,* he emphasizes that in addition to the transcendence of one's own body there is a transcendence of things from the perspective of human existence. Nevertheless, in this work such movements remain juxtaposed with one another, even though there are clearly cross-references. Now, on the contrary, the insertion of the body and things into the same ontological fabric, conceived diacritically, collapses the distinction between subject and object, as well as that between activity and passivity. This permits the determination of the source of transcendence in the very structure of Being. On this subject, therefore, Taminiaux remarks that in Merleau-Ponty's final writings "the very word 'transcendence' itself has changed its meaning; it no longer designates the intentional escape from what is simply given but, instead, a belonging to a Being that withholds itself, a Being at a distance, ever open, one that, more than being grasped by us, calls out to and holds us" (J. Taminiaux, "L'Expérience, l'expression et la forme dans l'itinéraire de Merleau-Ponty," in *Le Regard et l'excédent* [The Hague: Martinus Nijhoff, 1977], 110; "Experience, Expression, and Form in Merleau-Ponty's Itinerary," in *Dialectic and Difference,* ed. and trans. Robert Crease and James T. Decker [Atlantic Highlands, N.J.: Humanities, 1985], 149).

30. Consequently, while the preface of *Phenomenology of Perception* emphasized Husserl's merit at having distinguished operative intentionality from act intentionality, here Merleau-Ponty tends to underline how operative intentionality in Husserl remains inflexible because of a "*positivist* endeavor" (*VI* 285/231, Merleau-Ponty's emphasis). On the other hand, Merleau-Ponty's 1945 work was itself influenced by this endeavor. On the abandonment, in Merleau-Ponty's ontology, of the idea of a "phenomenological positivism" affirmed in *Phenomenology of Perception* (*PP* xii/xvii), see Taminiaux, *Le Regard et l'excédent,* 90–115; *Dialectic and Difference,* 131–54. See also G. B. Madison, *La Phénoménologie de Merleau-Ponty: Une recherche des limites de la conscience* (Paris: Klincksieck, 1973), 208–9; *The Phenomenology of Merleau-Ponty* (Athens: Ohio University Press, 1981), 195–96.

31. Cf. M. Merleau-Ponty, "Bergson se faisant," read at the Bergson Congress (May 17–20, 1959) and published in *Bulletin de la Société française de philosophie,* no. 1 (1960): 35–45; "Bergson in the Making," reprinted in *S* 229–41/182–91.

Regarding the influence of Bergson on Merleau-Ponty's later thought, see R. Ronchi, *Bergson filosofo dell'interpretazione* (Genova: Marietti, 1990), in particular chap. 3; E. Lisciani-Petrini, "Merleau-Ponty–Bergson: Un dialogo 'se faisant,'" *Il pensiero,* n.s., no. 33 (1993): 67–93; R. Barbaras, *Le Tournant de l'ex-*

périence (Paris: Vrin, 1998), in particular chap. 2; T. Toadvine, "Nature and Negation: Merleau-Ponty's Reading of Bergson," *Chiasmi International,* n.s., 2 (2000): 107–17.

32. "The present itself is not an absolute coincidence without transcendence; even the *Urerlebnis* involves not total coincidence, but partial coincidence, because it has horizons and would not be without them—the present, also, is ungraspable from close-up . . . it is an encompassing" (*VI* 249/195). See equally *VI* 244/191.

33. "But," Merleau-Ponty wonders, "what is a coincidence that is only partial? It is a coincidence always past or always future, an experience that remembers an impossible past, anticipates an impossible future, that emerges from Being or that will incorporate itself into Being, that 'is of it' but is not it, and therefore is not a coincidence, a real fusion, as of two positive terms or two elements of an alloyage, but an overlaying, as of a hollow and a relief which remain distinct" (*VI* 163–64/122–23).

34. For an examination of this theme, see M. Carbone, *La Visibilité de l'invisible: Merleau-Ponty entre Cézanne et Proust* (Hildesheim: Georg Olms, 2001), 17–31.

35. "In short: nothingness (or rather non-being) is hollow and not *hole*" (*VI* 249/196). Another working note adds: "The soul, the for-itself is *a hollow and not a void,* not absolute non-being with respect to a Being that would be plenitude and hard core. The sensibility of the others is 'the other side' of their aesthesiological body. And I can surmise this other side, *nichturpräsentierbar,* through the articulation of the other's body on *my sensible*" (*VI* 286/233). Regarding Merleau-Ponty's critique of the Sartrean conception of subjectivity, cf. also *VI* 78ff./ 52ff.

36. *The Visible and the Invisible* indicates that "[w]hen I find again the actual world such as it is, under my hands, under my eyes, up against my body, I find much more than an object: a Being of which my vision is a part, a visibility older than my operations or my acts" (*VI* 164/123).

37. It is necessary to recall concerning this issue the manner in which the course summary on "The Problem of Passivity" underlines that "sleeping consciousness is not a recess of pure nothingness: it is cluttered with the debris of the past and present; it plays with them" (*RC* 68/115–16).

38. "The 'associations' of psychoanalysis are in reality 'rays' of time and of the world" (*VI* 293/240). Another passage of *The Visible and the Invisible* explains in fact that "[l]ike the memory screen of the psychoanalysts, the present, the visible counts so much for me and has an absolute prestige for me only by reason of this immense latent content of the past, the future, and the elsewhere, which it announces and which it conceals" (*VI* 154/114). On this subject, see also Gambazzi, "Fenomenologia e psicoanalisi nell'ultimo Merleau-Ponty," esp. 122 n. 30.

39. Regarding this privilege that Merleau-Ponty attributes to speech in *Phenomenology of Perception,* see in particular the chapter of this work devoted to "The Body as Expression, and Speech" as well as the one devoted to "The Cogito."

40. "This notion of Time embodied, of years past but not separated from us, it was now my intention to emphasize as strongly as possible in my work. And

at this very moment, in the house of the Prince de Guermantes, as though to strengthen me in my resolve, the noise of my parents' footsteps as they accompanied M. Swann to the door and the peal—resilient, ferruginous, interminable, fresh and shrill—of the bell on the garden gate which informed me that at last he had gone and that mamma would presently come upstairs, these sounds rang again in my ears, yes, unmistakably I heard these very sounds, situated though they were in a remote past" (*R* 3:1046/1105).

41. Anne Simon also observes that this expression by Merleau-Ponty "makes one think of the final pages of *The Past Recaptured*" (Simon, "Proust et l''architecture' du visible," 106 n. 1).

The consonance of the Proustian figure of "embodied time" with the Merleau-Pontian conception of temporality moreover reveals the motifs demonstrated by Ricoeur's commentary on this figure: "The itinerary of *Remembrance* moves from the idea of a distance that separates to that of a distance that joins together. This is confirmed by the final figure of time proposed in *Remembrance,* that of an accumulated duration that is, in a sense, beneath us" (*Time and Narrative,* 2:224/151).

42. In fact, Giorgio Agamben notes that "Proust seems . . . to be thinking about certain twilight states, such as half-sleep and the loss of consciousness: 'I could not even be sure at first who I was'—such is its typical formulation, of which Poulet inventoried the innumerable variations" (G. Agamben, *Infanzia e storia: Distruzione dell'esperienza e origine della storia,* 2d ed. [Turin: Einaudi, 1979], 39).

43. On this topic, one must recall that Walter Benjamin, in his essay on Baudelaire, recognizes in Proust's work a critique of the concept of *Erlebnis,* to which he sees opposed that of *Erfahrung* as experience accumulated in passivity. Consequently, he brings the dialectic of memory and forgetfulness of which the *Remembrance* is woven back to this latter concept. See W. Benjamin, "Über einige Motive bei Baudelaire" (1939–40), in *Gesammelte Schriften,* vol. 1, bk. 2, ed. R. Tiedemann and H. Schweppenhäuser (Frankfurt am Main: Suhrkamp, 1972–77), 605–53; "On Some Motifs in Baudelaire," in *Illuminations,* trans. Harry Zohn (New York: Schocken Books, 1968), 155–200. See also W. Benjamin, "Zum Bilde Prousts" (1929), in *Gesammelte Schriften,* vol. 2, bk. 1, 310–25; "The Image of Proust," in *Illuminations,* 201–15.

We refer here to our *Di alcuni motivi in Marcel Proust* (Milan: Cortina, 1998), in which we have had occasion to compare the interpretations given by Benjamin and Merleau-Ponty on this subject.

Chapter 2

1. Merleau-Ponty's expression echoes this one from Pascal: "Se moquer de la philosophie, c'est vraiment philosopher," whose English translation reads precisely: "True philosophy scoffs at philosophy" (B. Pascal, *Pascal's Pensées* [1669], bilingual edition, trans. H. F. Stewart [London: Routledge and Kegan Paul, 1950], 498–99).

2. See respectively *NC* 33ff. and *RC* 141ff./167ff.

3. See, for example, *VI* 219/165 and *VI* 236–37/183.

4. A few pages before the one we just quoted, Merleau-Ponty affirms: "With Hegel something comes to an end. After Hegel, there is a philosophical void. This is not to say there has been a lack of thinkers or of geniuses, but that Marx, Kierkegaard, and Nietzsche start from a denial of philosophy" (*RC* 141–42/168). On this subject, see also *NC* 38.

5. Lefort too emphasizes this second thought: "Dans l'introduction aux leçons de 1959, Merleau-Ponty écartait l'idée d'interroger notre état de non-philosophie par un examen de Kierkegaard, Nietzsche et Marx. Ce serait, disait-il, déboucher sur le constat que la métaphysique s'achève avec Hegel et se demander seulement si les trois penseurs qui se sont détachés de lui ont vraiment rompu avec elle et dans quelle mesure ils annoncent les problèmes de notre temps. Il préferait aller droit à ces problèmes. Néanmoins, son second cours de 1961 rouvre la voie qu'il semblait avoir abandonnée" (C. Lefort, "Préface" to *NC* 24–25).

6. With regard to this topic, in fact, Merleau-Ponty speaks of "a 'negative philosophy' (in the sense of 'negative theology')" (*NC* 275/9): the same terms by which he defined, in a working note of *The Visible and the Invisible* dated February 1959, the framework of the new ontology that this work should have elaborated (see *VI* 233/179). This confirms that the question on which this course focuses formed at that time the very heart of Merleau-Ponty's thought, as Lefort emphasized in his short "Présentation" of the preparatory notes as well as in the article entitled "Philosophie et non-philosophie," *Esprit* no. 66 (June 1982): 101, 106.

7. See M. Heidegger, *Hegels Begriff der Erfahrung* (1942–43), in *Holzwege* (Frankfurt am Main: Klostermann, 1950), 105–92; issued separately in English as *Hegel's Concept of Experience* (*with a Section from Hegel's "Phenomenology of Spirit" in the Kenley Royce Dove Translation*) (New York: Harper and Row, 1970). Information about the use Merleau-Ponty makes of the text of the "Einleitung" reproduced in Heidegger's essay can be found in Lefort's "Présentation" of these preparatory notes (see *NC* 272). Comparisons between Heidegger's and Merleau-Ponty's commentaries on the "Introduction" have been made by Hugh J. Silverman, *Inscriptions: After Phenomenology and Structuralism,* 2d ed. (Evanston: Northwestern University Press, 1997), 108ff., as well as by S. Mancini, *Sempre di nuovo: Merleau-Ponty e la dialettica dell'espressione,* 2d ed. (Milan: Mimesis, 2001), 179ff.

8. The same paragraphs are numbered 85–89 in *Hegel's Phenomenology of Spirit,* trans. A. V. Miller (New York: Oxford University Press, 1977), 54–57.

9. See *NC* 316/49–50 and *NC* 320/53. More precisely, the title "Einleitung" ("Introduction"), even if it actually doesn't appear at the beginning of these pages, comes afterward in the index to indicate the fact that it was already present in the first edition of the work.

10. We are indeed reminded of a working note of *The Visible and the Invisible* dated November 1960, in which Merleau-Ponty records his intention of moving from the concept of chiasm in order to "elaborate an idea of philosophy" (*VI* 319/266). With regard to this working note, see the beginning of our chapter 4.

11. As is well known, this expression was at first to have been the title for *The Visible and the Invisible.* We have here recalled it in order to stress the judgment of Lefort, according to which Merleau-Ponty's commentary on Hegel's pages "s'inscrit dans un travail d'auto-interprétation" (C. Lefort, "Présentation" to *NC* 273).

12. "When Husserl insistently says that phenomenological reflection begins in the natural attitude . . . this is not just a way of saying that we must necessarily begin with and go by way of opinion before we can attain knowledge. The doxa of the natural attitude is an Urdoxa. To what is fundamental and original in theoretical consciousness it opposes what is fundamental and original in our existence. Its rights of priority are definitive, and reduced consciousness must take them into account" (*S* 207/164).

13. A little below, Merleau-Ponty explains that "metaphysics here is nothing other than a taking possession of what appears" (*NC* 286/19).

14. See *VI* 48ff./28ff., esp. 51/30.

15. See *VI* 57/35.

16. Concerning the reference to Hegel, see, for example, G. W. F. Hegel, *Enzyklopädie der philosophischen Wissenschaften im Grundrisse* (1830); *The Encyclopaedia Logic: Part I of the Encyclopaedia of Philosophical Sciences with the Zusätze,* trans. T. F. Geraets, W. A. Suchting, and H. S. Harris (Indianapolis: Hackett, 1991), §84.

17. See *VI* 53/34–35.

18. See *VI* 252/199.

19. See *NC* 286/19.

20. See *NC* 285/18. See also *NC* 297, where Hegel's phrase is interpreted as a reaffirmation of the intrinsic bond that joins appearance and the absolute.

21. "Sans doute"—Lefort observes—"peut-on dire qu'il projette dans Hegel ses propres questions; mais il nous donne tout autant l'impression de les avoir apprises à son contact" (Lefort, "Philosophie et non-philosophie," 111).

22. *PG,* "Einleitung," §14. See *Hegel's Phenomenology of Spirit,* trans. A. V. Miller, §86, 55.

23. See *NC* 303–4/38.

24. See *VI* 67/43.

25. As we know, the famous phrase with which the manuscript of *The Visible and the Invisible* ends speaks of "two aspects of the reversibility which is the ultimate truth" (*VI* 204/155).

26. See *NC* 316/50 and *NC* 319/52.

27. See *NC* 319/52.

28. See *NC* 288/21. On the conception of subjectivity as *fissure* in this last phase of Merleau-Ponty's thought, see chap. 1, "Time and Subject."

29. This conception of the Irrelative is, of course, another way to describe the "mutation of the relationship between humanity and Being" that Merleau-Ponty feels in our epoch. Indeed, in his conclusion to the essay "The Philosopher and His Shadow," Merleau-Ponty writes: "This renewal of the world is also mind [*esprit*]'s renewal, a rediscovery of that brute mind which, untamed by any culture, is asked to create culture anew. From then on the irrelative is not nature

in itself, not the system of absolute consciousness's apprehensions, nor man either, but that 'teleology' Husserl speaks about which is written and thought about in parentheses—that jointing and framing of Being which is being realized through man" (*S* 228/181).

30. *PG,* "Absolut Wissen," §21. See *Hegel's Phenomenology of Spirit,* trans. A. V. Miller, §808, 492.

31. This judgment, which is also explicitly quoted (see *NC* 317 and 320), argues that in the *Phenomenology of Spirit* Hegel seems to conceive phenomenology as "the *whole of the system* from a certain point of view" (J. Hyppolite, *Genèse et structure de la Phénoménologie de l'Esprit de Hegel* [Paris: Aubier-Montaigne, 1946], 2:582 n. 3; *Genesis and Structure of "Hegel's Phenomenology of Spirit,"* trans. Samuel Cherniak and John Heckman [Evanston: Northwestern University Press, 1974], 605 n. 29), while "in the *Encyclopaedia* . . . the *Phenomenology* will then only have a specific place" (ibid.). The influence of this second statement on these preparatory notes will be evident later.

32. See *Hegel's Phenomenology of Spirit,* trans. A. V. Miller, §87, 55–56.

33. See *NC* 292/26.

34. See *PG,* "Einleitung," §13.

35. See *NC* 291/26 and *NC* 302/37.

36. *PG,* "Einleitung," §14.

37. See *NC* 306 n. b/307–8 n. 62.

38. This is the term he employs (see *NC* 313/47), but he will notice in the following pages its inadequacy (see *NC* 319/52).

39. This paragraph coincides with §§88–89 in *Hegel's Phenomenology of Spirit,* trans. A. V. Miller, 56–57.

40. See *NC* 316/49.

41. See also *NC* 320/53.

42. See *NC* 313 n. a/309 n. 72. Concerning Merleau-Ponty's judgment about the relation between, on the one hand, Hegel's *Phänomenologie des Geistes* (1807), and, on the other, his *Wissenschaft der Logik* (1812–16) and *Enzyklopädie der philosophischen Wissenschaften im Grundrisse* (1817, 1827, 1830), it is worth noting what Jacques Taminiaux said about an analogous judgment expressed by Merleau-Ponty in the essay entitled "Hegel's Existentialism" ("L'existentialisme chez Hegel," [1946], reprinted in *SNS*): "First of all, any allegation of a supposed opposition between the Hegel of 1807 and of 1827 disregards the fact that the architectonic and the conceptual apparatus of the so-called mature system were both established at the time of the Jena writings. Furthermore, this thesis silently overlooks Hegel's stated project of this period: the realization of an absolute idealism. Finally, it conflicts with the most recent results of the *Hegelforschung,* which tend to show that a preestablished logic does indeed found the articulation of the *Phenomenology of Spirit.* But if Merleau-Ponty's proposition cannot be justified by appealing to Hegel's writings, it may be justified by appealing to those of Merleau-Ponty" (J. Taminiaux, "Merleau-Ponty de la dialectique à l'hyperdialectique," in *Recoupements* [Brussels: Ousia, 1982], 100; "Merleau-Ponty: From Dialectic to Hyperdialectic," in *Dialectic and Difference,* 160–61).

43. See *NC* 309/43 and *NC* 311/45.

44. See *NC* 318/52.

45. See *NC* 341/73.

46. This is also the opinion of C. Lefort, "Préface" to *NC* 27.

47. See, for example, *VI* 55/33.

48. Concerning this term, see, for example, *NC* 339/73.

49. Lefort appropriately underlines that "quand le philosophe prend en charge la question de la réversibilité, du chiasme, il ne peut s'en délivrer pour en faire l'objet du savoir. Lui-même ne saurait occuper la position du pur spectateur, qui permettrait de surplomber les *deux côtés* de toute expérience, de formuler, comme Hegel, l'identité de l'identité et de la non-identité" (Lefort, "Philosophie et non-philosophie," 110).

50. Here are Hegel's words: "We see clearly that both are the same; but what is essential is to retain for the whole investigation the fact that the two moments, *Concept and Object, being-for-another* and *being-for-itself,* themselves fall within the knowledge which we are studying. We therefore do not need to bring along standards or to apply our preconceived ideas and thoughts throughout the entire course of the investigation. On the contrary, in leaving them along the way, we come to examine them as the thing is in-itself and for-itself" (*PG,* "Einleitung," §12). See also *Hegel's Phenomenology of Spirit,* trans. A. V. Miller, §84, 53–54.

51. We ourselves translated the last quoted phrase, which does not appear in the English version.

52. See *PG,* "Einleitung," §17. Merleau-Ponty emphasizes the use of this term (see *NC* 313/47 and 314/47).

53. See *NC* 305/39–40.

54. *The Visible and the Invisible* argues indeed that "[p]hilosophy is the perceptual faith questioning itself about itself" (*VI* 139/103).

55. We use the clarifying distinction between "cognition" and "knowledge" even if both terms translate here Merleau-Ponty's single word *connaissance.*

56. See *VI* 256/202 and *VI* 314–15/260–61.

57. See *VI* 257/204.

58. Referring to the implications of this definition, Merleau-Ponty explains that "This 1) does not realize a surpassing, a dialectic in the Hegelian sense; 2) is realized on the spot, by encroachment, thickness, *spatiality*" (*VI* 318/264). With regard to this last reference to spatiality, and in connection with the conception of the *Vorhabe* of Being, there is another working note that is clarifying, although it concerns a different topic: "The *Vorhabe* of place by my body that betakes itself unto that place" (*VI* 255/201). With regard to the problem of a new definition of the identity requested by the idea that "the mediating term and the mediated term . . . are the 'same,'" see again *VI* 126ff./92ff.

59. See *VI* 137/101, as well as *VI* 200–202/152–54 and *VI* 256/203.

60. See *NC* 317ff./49ff.

61. See *VI* 125–30/91–95, but also, as another example, the characterization of "hyper-reflection" (*VI* 61/38).

62. For example, in the phrase where he remarks that dialectic is "*essentially and by definition unstable,* so that it has never been able to formulate itself

into theses without denaturing itself, and . . . if one wishes to maintain its spirit it is perhaps necessary to not even name it." And again, on the same page, when he adds that the dialectic "is in danger of becoming [a signification cut off from the experience of being] as soon as it is stated *in theses, in univocal significations,* as soon as it is *detached from its antepredicative context*" (*VI* 126/92, emphases added). As we will try to explain, this assimilation is dictated by the reason why in *a certain* categorial horizon (or, in other terms, in a certain *ontology*), every formulation of the dialectic cannot but be thetic. As a matter of fact, in the preparatory notes for the course dated 1958–59, Merleau-Ponty explains that to him the contemporary "décadence de la philosophie est *inessentielle;* est celle d'*une certaine manière de philosopher* (selon substance, subjet-objet, causalité). La philosophie trouvera aide dans la poésie, art, etc., dans un rapport beaucoup plus étroit avec elles, elle renaîtra et réinterprétera ainsi son propre passé de métaphysique—qui n'est pas passé" (*NC* 39, emphases added).

63. In this sense, Lefort advises that such a remark "indique la direction de la question de Merleau-Ponty et sa limite—celle à laquelle il se heurte lui-même" (Lefort, "Philosophie et non-philosophie," 111).

64. See *VI* 319/266.

65. "No absolute pure philosophical word" (*VI* 319/102).

66. In the sense indicated by this other passage of *The Visible and the Invisible:* "The words most charged with philosophy are not necessarily those that contain what they say, but rather those that most energetically open upon Being, because they more closely convey the life of the whole and make our habitual evidences vibrate until they disjoin. Hence it is a question whether philosophy as reconquest of brute or wild being can be accomplished by the resources of eloquent language, or whether it would not be necessary for philosophy to use language in a way that takes from it its power of immediate or direct signification in order to equal it with what it wishes all the same to say" (*VI* 139/102).

67. In *Eye and Mind,* Merleau-Ponty significantly defines the sensible universe as "the oneiric world of analogy" (*OE* 41/132).

68. We will try to explore all of these problems in greater depth in our last chapter.

69. "The choice is between it and a dogmatism of reflection concerning which we know only too well where it goes, since with it philosophy concludes the moment it begins and, for this very reason, does not make us comprehend our own obscurity" (*VI* 62/39).

70. For a discussion of the history of the reception of Plato's anecdote concerning Talete and the maidservant from Thrace, and its contemporary implications, see Hans Blumenberg, *Das Lachen der Thrakerin: Eine Urgeschichte der Theorie* (Frankfurt am Main: Suhrkamp, 1987).

Chapter 3

1. See *RC* 141/167.

2. Moreover, this is implicitly confirmed by the summary of the course whose English title is "Philosophy as Interrogation." In this summary Merleau-

Ponty announces: "we have decided to postpone until next year the continuation of the study we began on the ontology of nature, and to devote this year to some general reflections on the meaning of this inquiry and the question of the possibility of philosophy today" (*RC* 141/167). See also the corresponding *NC* 37–38.

3. Upon introducing these lectures, Merleau-Ponty states: "the purpose of this course is to try to formulate philosophically our ontology, which remains implicit, in the air, and to do it through the contrast with Cartesian ontology (Descartes and successors)" (*NC* 166).

4. Merleau-Ponty claims, in fact, that "[t]here is a circular relation between Being and beings. We must take hold again of a common life between essence and existence" (*N* 180/134). On this subject, see also the entire chapter entitled "Interrogation and Intuition" of *VI* 142–71/105–29.

5. It is important to recall that, according to Merleau-Ponty, "Darwinian thought" is "the artificialist philosophy . . . in its most developed forms," since it is based both on an "ultra-mechanism" and an "ultra-finalism" (*RC* 136/165, trans. modified).

6. Confronting what Uexküll theorizes in *Umwelt und Innenwelt der Tiere* (Berlin: Springer, 1909) and in *Streifzüge durch die Umwelten von Tieren und Menschen—Ein Bilderbuch unsichtbarer Welten* (Berlin: Springer, 1934), Merleau-Ponty observes: "These two interpretations of the *Natursubjekt* are not what is most interesting in the work of Uexküll. The first only takes up the Kantian solution again, the second the intuitions of Schelling. . . . There is however, something new: the notion of *Umwelt*" (*N* 232/177).

An introduction to the most important stages of Uexküll's philosophical reflection appears in Mondella's preface to the most recent Italian edition of the second text cited above: see J. von Uexküll, *Ambiente e comportamento,* Italian trans. P. Manfredi (Milan: Il Saggiatore, 1967), 9–77.

7. "We must admit in the very fabric of the physical elements a transtemporal and transspatial element of which we do not take account by supposing an essence outside of time" (*N* 230/176). Merleau-Ponty synthesizes shortly below in the text: "The notion of *Umwelt* no longer allows us to consider the organism in its relation to the exterior world, as an effect of the exterior world, or as a cause. The *Umwelt* is not presented in front of the animal like a goal; it is not present like an idea" (*N* 233/178).

8. J. von Uexküll, quoted by Merleau-Ponty (*N* 228/173, trans. modified). Merleau-Ponty quoted Uexküll's statement already in *SC* 172/159, taking it from the article by F. Buytendijk, "Les Différences essentielles des fonctions psychiques chez l'homme et les animaux," *Cahiers de philosophie de la nature* 4 (1930): 131.

9. These are the pages in which Proust describes Swann as having reached the consideration of the "musical *motifs* as actual ideas" (*R* 1:349/379).

10. In this quotation, it is evident how Merleau-Ponty connects the musical meaning and the biological meaning of the term "theme."

11. On the importance of this question (given what we will later conclude, we could say that its relevance is *ontological*), Merleau-Ponty states: "[h]ow are we to understand, then, this relation between the totality and the parts? What status

must we give totality? Such is the philosophical question that Coghill's experiments pose, a question which is at the center of this course on the idea of Nature and maybe of every philosophy" (*N* 194/145, trans. modified).

12. Mondella moreover underlines how Uexküll's work is to be placed in the background of a crisis of biology which rendered problematic the meaning of terms such as "variation," immobilized between causalism and finalism: "Were the variations a casual and passive process, determined by external factors, or the result of an internal tendency of the organism which manifests itself in its adaptation to the environment?" (Mondella, "Introduzione" to Uexküll, *Ambiente e comportamento,* 14).

13. For the expression to which we are referring, see note 29 of the previous chapter.

It is interesting to point out that Deleuze and Guattari have also in turn underlined that Uexküll's conception "*n'est pas une conception finaliste, mais mélodique*" (G. Deleuze and F. Guattari, *Qu'est-ce que la philosophie?* [Paris: Minuit, 1991], 176, emphasis added).

14. We quote the passage in its entirety: "[a]t the end of the experience produced by this ontology [i.e., the Cartesian one] European philosophy again confronts nature as an oriented and blind productivity. This does not represent a return to teleology. Properly speaking, teleology understood as the conformity of the event to a concept shares the same fate as mechanism—these are both concepts of *artificialism.* Natural production has to be understood in some other way" (*RC* 117/151).

15. This statement, made about "Portmann's study of the animal appearance" (see *N* 244ff/186ff.), refers to the common inspiration that, according to Merleau-Ponty, underlies the biological studies considered in his own lectures devoted to "the study of animal behavior" (see *N* 220ff/166ff.).

16. For example, he notes that "London and Bauer . . . see in quantum mechanics a 'theory of species,' and they put in doubt the idea that every object has an individual existence" (*N* 128/92).

17. See *OE* 41/132.

18. In *Eye and Mind,* the English translation renders voyance as "visualization."

19. See *NC* 391. Merleau-Ponty synthesizes shortly below: "[a]ll considered Proust: the carnal essences; Valéry: the conscience is not within the immanence, but within the life; Claudel: the simultaneity, the most real is *beneath* us; St J Perse: the Poetry as an awakening to the Being; Cl. Simon: the zone of credulity and the zone of the sensible being.

"There is an overturning of the relationships between the visible and the invisible, the flesh and the mind; a discovery of a signification as nervure of the full Being; an overcoming of the insularity of the minds" (*NC* 392).

20. G. Charbonnier, *Le Monologue du peintre I* (Paris: Julliard, 1959), 34. Max Ernst's statement is already echoed in *VI* 261/208, and is quoted in *OE* 30–31/128–29. On this subject, see Carbone, *La Visibilité de l'invisible,* 110–18.

21. In its full ontological significance, it is necessary to understand as follows the meaning of "simultaneity" established by *Eye and Mind:* "beings that are

different, 'exterior,' foreign to one another, are yet absolutely *together*" (*OE* 84/146).

Regarding the literary expression of simultaneity, as we indicated in note 15 of the first chapter, Merleau-Ponty considers it particularly in the conclusive sentence of the *Remembrance* (about which, see *NC* 197). As the quotation in note 19 of the present chapter shows, he finds it in the pages of Claudel (see *NC* 198ff.) and in those of Simon (see *NC* 204ff.) as well.

22. See *NC* 170 and 173, as well as *Eye and Mind,* where it is emphasized that the "extraordinary overlapping [*empiétement*]" between vision and movement "forbids us to conceive of vision as an operation of thought that would set up before the mind a picture or a representation of the world" (*OE* 17/124). David Michael Levin recalls that "like Heidegger, Merleau-Ponty uses phenomenology to contest the history of metaphysics, which has reduced the thing to an object, reduced human beings to subjects, and posited the object it has artificially constructed within a structure of representation (*Vor-stellung*) that relates it to a disembodied subject" (D. M. Levin, *The Philosopher's Gaze: Modernity in the Shadows of Enlightenment* [Berkeley and Los Angeles: University of California Press, 1999], 201). Christine Buci-Glucksmann points out in turn that by the notion of *voyance,* Merleau-Ponty elaborates "a Seeing which exceeds the sight, a visual freed from the only optic-representative frame" (C. Buci-Glucksmann, *La Folie du voir: De l'esthétique baroque* [Paris: Galilée, 1986], 70).

23. As we know, Merleau-Ponty significantly defines the sensible universe as "the oneiric world of analogy" in *Eye and Mind* (*OE* 41/132).

24. See E. Husserl, *Formale und transzendentale Logik: Versuch einer Kritik der logischen Vernunft,* ed. P. Janssen, in *Husserliana,* vol. 17 (The Hague: Martinus Nijhoff, 1974), 257. Originally published in *Jahrbuch für Philosophie und phänomenologische Forschung* 10 (1929).

It ought to be remembered that Rimbaud, in turn, came to theorize the becoming *voyant* of the poet "by a long, gigantic, and rational *derangement* of *all the senses*" (A. Rimbaud, "Lettre du voyant" [to Paul Demeny, written May 15, 1871], in A. Rimbaud, *Complete Works, Selected Letters,* ed. W. Fowlie [Chicago and London: The University of Chicago Press, 1966], 307, upon which Merleau-Ponty comments: "This does not mean not to think anymore—the derangement of the senses is the breaking down of barriers between themselves in order to find again their undivision—And therefore *not my thinking, but theirs*" (*NC* 186, emphasis added).

25. *VI* 272/218. Here the specific reference is to Paul Klee's painting, as we can conclude from *NC* 56, where Merleau-Ponty again uses the expression "skin of things," this time speaking explicitly of Klee.

As for the parallelism between contemporary music and painting, Merleau-Ponty develops it in *NC* 61–64. See esp. *NC* 61–62: "Generalization (and 'purification') of music as well as of painting: there were some privileged forms of tonality. . . . All this [is] not physically suppressed, but rather reintegrated into [a] wider range of musical possibility, according to which the privileged structures constitute only a few of the possible variants of the 12-tone series."

26. See the letter written to Mersenne on November 20, 1629, in R. Descartes, *Oeuvres philosophiques,* ed. F. Alquié (Paris: Bordas, 1998), 1:227–32.

27. This equivalence was previously claimed in *OE* 44 n.13/389 n. 22: "[t]he system of means by which painting makes us see is a scientific matter. Why, then, do we not methodically produce perfect images of the world, arriving at a universal art purged of personal art, just as the universal language would free us of all the confused relationships that lurk in existent languages?"

28. See *NC* 189.

29. See *NC* 186 and, about the quotation from Rimbaud, the letter "À Georges Izambard" (May [13], 1871), which is considered a draft of the "Lettre du voyant," in Rimbaud, *Complete Works, Selected Letters,* 305.

30. Regarding this, he asks himself: "[i]s it not a general conception of ideas?" and shortly below: "[t]hey said Platonism, but these ideas are without an intelligible sun" (*NC* respectively 193 and 194).

31. For the reference here and hereafter to the Proustian pages, see *R* 1:349–50/379–81.

32. We already discussed the commentary that *The Visible and the Invisible* develops on these pages in the fifth chapter of our *La Visibilité de l'invisible,* to which the reader can refer.

33. See *VI* 198/151.

34. In this perspective, moreover, we could read the overall inspiration that progressively orients the theories of Uexküll, who—Mondella claims—"in his last years of study, tried more and more to express the knowledge of the harmonic plan which realizes itself in the unity between the animal subject and the individual world, as the knowledge of a 'meaning.' This means the knowledge of a relation which is not expressible through a connection between cause and effect, but rather between the entirety and its parts. Such a relation of the entirety and its parts is not explainable, according to the author, through *any abstract knowledge of a conceptual kind, but rather it is obtainable,* as we have seen, *through a form of perceptual knowledge*" (Mondella, "Introduzione" to Uexküll, *Ambiente e comportamento,* 69, emphases added).

35. "We are not here proposing any empiricist genesis of thought: we are asking precisely what is that central vision that joins the scattered visions, . . . that *I think* that must be able to accompany all our experiences. We are proceeding toward the center, we are seeking to comprehend how there is a center, what the unity consists of, we are not saying that it is a sum or a result" (*VI* 191/145).

36. As we saw in our first chapter, with this term ("initiation") Merleau-Ponty translates the Husserlian concept of *Stiftung,* which, in his opinion, designates "the unlimited fecundity of each present which, precisely because it is singular and passes, can never stop having been and thus being universally" (*S* 73–74/59), exactly because once and for all that present inaugurated a *dimension* pregnant with promises and anticipations.

37. Here he echoes what Uexküll stated, for example, in 1909: "[i]n a melody there is a reciprocal influence between the first and the last tone, and we can therefore say that the last tone is possible only because of the first, but, in the same way, that the first is possible only because of the last. The procedure is the same for the formation of the structure in plants and animals" (Uexküll, *Umwelt und Innenwelt der Tiere,* 23–24).

The aspect of *anticipation* that Merleau-Ponty perceives in the *beginning* is clarified in a note that he writes on music—understood "as the model of meaning"—during the period of his thinking that we are examining. He writes: "While listening to beautiful music: the impression that this movement that starts up is already at its endpoint, which it is going to have been, or [that it is] sinking into the future that we have a hold of as well as the past—although we cannot say exactly what it will be. Anticipated retrospection—Retrograde movement *in futuro:* it comes down towards me entirely done" (M. Merleau-Ponty, "Deux notes inédites sur la musique"; "Two Unpublished Notes on Music," trans. Leonard Lawlor, *Chiasmi International,* n.s., 3 [2001]: 18). For Merleau-Ponty, therefore, if in the *beginning* one can perceive the *entirety,* this happens by virtue of that "retrograde movement *in futuro*" that, given its character, already prefigures and implies the *reprise* of the anticipation.

38. "It is in this way that things happen in the construction of a living being. There is no priority of effect over cause. Just as we cannot say that the last note is the end of the melody of it, and the first is the effect neither can we, distinguish the sense apart from the sense in which the melody expresses itself" (*N* 228/174, trans. modified).

39. In reference to the theories of E. S. Russell and R. Ruyer, and even to those of Uexküll, Merleau-Ponty synthesizes: "[o]ne can, therefore, speak of a presence of the theme of these realizations or say that *the events are grouped around a certain absence:* thus, in perception, the vertical and the horizontal are given everywhere and present nowhere. Totality is likewise everywhere and nowhere" (*N* 239–40/183, trans. modified, emphasis added). Furthermore, we have already seen Merleau-Ponty compare the "orientation" which underlies animal behavior, according to Uexküll, with that "of our oneiric consciousness toward certain poles that *are never seen for themselves,* but which are, however, directly the cause of all the elements of a dream" (*N* 233/178, emphasis added).

40. This excess is indicated by Proust, who emphasizes that "[w]hen he [i.e., Swann] had sought to disentangle from his confused impressions how it was that it [i.e., the little phrase] swept over and enveloped him, he had observed that it was to the closeness of the intervals between the five notes which composed it and to the constant repetition of two of them that was due that impression of a frigid and withdrawn sweetness; but in reality he knew that he was basing this conclusion not upon the phrase itself, but merely upon certain equivalents, substituted (for his mind's convenience) for the mysterious entity of which he had become aware . . . when for the first time he had heard the sonata played" (*R* 1:349/380). For Merleau-Ponty's commentary on this passage, see *VI* 197/150, as well as *NC* 193–95; both texts find in this passage a description of the relationship between "sensible ideas" and "ideas of the intelligence." Therefore, Proust seems to describe here a double excess: that of "sensible ideas" with respect to their presentation, but also with respect to their conceptualization.

41. P. Gambazzi, "La piega e il pensiero: Sull'ontologia di Merleau-Ponty," *Aut Aut* n.s., nos. 262–63 (1994): 28.

42. For the characterization of the relationship between the sensible and the intelligible that we have synthesized here, see in particular the working notes of *The Visible and the Invisible* entitled "The 'senses'—dimensionality—Being"

and "Problem of the negative and of the concept, Gradient," respectively dated November 1959 and February 1960, in *VI* 271–72/217–19 and 290–91/236–38. For our own commentary on these working notes, see our next chapter.

43. "We do not possess the musical or sensible ideas, precisely because they are negativity or absence circumscribed; they possess us" (*VI* 198–99/151).

44. On this subject, we are reminded of the critique of Husserl's "myth" of a disincarnated *Wesensschau* operated by a "pure spectator"—a critique that Merleau-Ponty develops in the previously quoted chapter "Interrogation and Intuition" of *The Visible and the Invisible* (see *VI,* esp. 155/116). Moreover, in a working note of the same text, he writes: "seeing is this sort of thought that has no need to think in order to possess the *Wesen*" (VI 301/247).

Thus, if Buci-Glucksmann wrote that "the *voyance*—which renders present to us what is absent—defines at the same time *the place of art and the access to Being,* the simultaneous arising of an aesthetics and of an 'ontology'" (Buci-Glucksmann, *La Folie du voir,* 71), at the same time we can also see a gnosiology emerging here, for Merleau-Ponty also defines by *voyance* a *Wesensschau* of carnal essences: "a *totally virtual Wesensschau* and, at the same time, *always already working* in the intuition (or in the vision, or, more generally, in the apprehension) of this or that phenomenon" (M. Richir, *Phénomènes, temps et êtres. Ontologie et phénoménologie* [Grenoble: Millon, 1987], 79).

45. In relation to the synesthetic configuration of *Wesensschau* that Merleau-Ponty seems to propose, we should not forget that he also characterizes it "as auscultation or palpation in depth" (*VI* 170/128). In addition, as to the problem of the unity of the senses, it should be pointed out that to conceive such a unity does not imply the presupposition of their original indifferentiation, but instead points out that *Transponierbarkeit* for which "each 'sense' is a 'world,' i.e., absolutely incommunicable for the other senses, and yet constructing a *something* which, through its structure, is from the very first *open* upon the world of the other senses, and with them forms one sole Being" (*VI* 271/217).

46. This deals with Claudel's *L'Oeil écoute* (Paris: Gallimard, 1946). Regarding Merleau-Ponty's observations, see *NC* 198–201.

Chapter 4

1. See, in particular, *VI* 200/153, where Merleau-Ponty also writes: "[i]t is as though the *visibility* that animates the sensible world were to emigrate" (emphasis added) into that of language, "as though it were to change flesh."

2. With regard to the persistence of "horizonal structures" in the algorithm, see also *PM* 149–52/105–7, as well as, in the same work, the entire chapter entitled "The Algorithm and the Mystery of Language," esp. *PM* 175/125, where, in contrast to the Platonism which underlies the pretense of mathematical thought to being "the reflection of an intelligible world," it is asserted that the series of whole numbers "is at each moment nothing but the ensemble of relations established within it *plus an open horizon of relations that can be constructed.*" Here, the reference is to Gauss's formula which gives the sum of a finite number of terms of an arithmetic progression. This formula is phenomenologically ex-

amined by Merleau-Ponty following the example of M. Wertheimer's text, *Productive Thinking* (New York and London: Harper and Brothers, 1945). This text is also mentioned in *The Visible and the Invisible,* immediately after the annotation that "the *Gestalt* contains the key to the problem of the mind" (*VI* 246/192).

3. See R. Barbaras, "Le Dédoublement de l'originaire," in Merleau-Ponty, *Notes de cours sur "L'Origine de la géométrie" suivi de recherches sur la phénoménologie de Merleau-Ponty,* ed. Renaud Barbaras (Paris: P.U.F., 1998), 289–303.

With regard to this problem, it also needs to be remembered how *The Prose of the World* defines "the perceived object" as the "prototype of meaning" of "what is understood" (*PM* 151/106) and how *The Visible and the Invisible,* in turn, defines "carnal being" as the "prototype of Being" (*VI* 179/136). Taminiaux also comments: "[t]hinking does not require that one leave the sensible to move to the intellectual, it requires that the individual reflect and retrieve the intertwining structures that are the very ones at work in the sensible" (J. Taminiaux, "Le Penseur et le peintre: Sur Merleau-Ponty," *La Part de l'oeil,* no. 7 [1991]: 42; "The Thinker and the Painter," trans. Michael Gendre, in *Merleau-Ponty Vivant,* ed. Martin C. Dillon [Albany: State University of New York Press, 1991], 203). According to Merleau-Ponty, then, the conceptless cohesion of the flesh and its diacriticity are not confined in the sphere of the sensible.

4. "Language in forming itself expresses, at least laterally, an ontogenesis of which is a part" (*VI* 139/102).

5. With regard to Husserl's statement of the complex of experience in terms of relations between layers, a working note in *The Visible and the Invisible* claims: "The relation between circularities (my body-the sensible) does not present the difficulties that the relation between 'layers' or linear orders presents (nor the immanence-transcendent alternative)

"In *Ideen II,* Husserl, 'disentangle' 'unravel' what is entangled The idea of chiasm and *Ineinander* is on the contrary the idea that every analysis that *disentangles* renders unintelligible— . . . It is a question of creating a new type of intelligibility (intelligibility through the world and Being as they are—'vertical' and not *horizontal*)" (*VI* 321–22/268). And another working note shortly after restates: "there is no *hierarchy* of orders or layers or planes (always founded on the individual-essence distinction), there is dimensionality of every fact and facticity of every dimension" (*VI* 324/270).

With particular reference to the first working note we quoted here, I. Matos Dias maintains: "[t]he classical problem of the division and the hierarchy between the sensible and the intelligible transforms itself when it is considered within the horizon of the flesh. . . . It is possible to interpret the relationship between the sensible and the intelligible like a reciprocal contamination and impregnation" (I. Matos Dias, *Maurice Merleau-Ponty: Une Esthésiologie ontologique,* in Merleau-Ponty, *Notes de cours sur "L'Origine de la géométrie" suivi de recherches sur la phénoménologie de Merleau-Ponty,* 279).

6. "What is proper to the sensible (as to language) is to be representative of the whole, not by a sign-signification relation, or by the immanence of the parts in one other and in the whole, but because each part is *torn up* from the

whole, comes with its roots, encroaches upon the whole, transgresses the frontiers of the others" (*VI* 271/218).

7. In another working note, in which Merleau-Ponty explains the reasoning contained in the note we just quoted, he says, "[s]ensoriality: for example, a color: yellow; it surpasses itself of itself: as soon as it becomes the color of the illumination, the dominant color of the field, it ceases to be such a color, it has therefore of itself an ontological function, it becomes apt to represent all things. . . . With one sole movement it imposes itself as particular and ceases to be visible as particular. . . . Now this particularity of the color, of the yellow, and this universality are not a *contradiction,* are *together* sensoriality itself: it is by the same virtue that the color, the yellow, at the same time gives itself as a *certain* being and as a *dimension,* the expression of *every possible being*— . . . this is not a contradiction, for it is precisely within its particularity as yellow and through it that the yellow becomes a universe or an *element*" (*VI* 271–72/217–18).

8. See chapter 3, "*Voyance.*"

9. In addition: "[t]he concept, the signification are the singular *dimensionalized,* the *formulated* structure" (*VI* 291/237).

10. "Partout et nulle part" is composed of six sections. These six sections originally constituted the preface and the introductions to five chapters of the collective work *Les Philosophes célèbres,* ed. M. Merleau-Ponty (Paris: Mazenod, 1956). Reprinted in *S* 158–200/126–58.

11. See note 43 of the previous chapter.

12. See the paragraph entitled "Kants Lehre vom Schönen. Ihre Mißdeutung durch Schopenhauer und Nietzsche," in M. Heidegger, *Nietzsche,* vol.1 (Pfullingen: Günther Neske, 1961); "Kant's Doctrine of the Beautiful: Its Misinterpretation by Schopenhauer and Nietzsche," in *Nietzsche,* vol. 1, *The Will to Power as Art,* trans. David Farrell Krell (New York: Harper and Row, 1979), 107–14.

13. Heidegger, *Nietzsche,* 1:108, emphasis added.

14. Ibid.

15. Ibid., 109, emphases added.

16. Ibid., emphasis added.

17. Ibid., emphases added.

18. Ibid., 110.

19. Ibid., 109, emphasis added. The German says: "Seinlassen des Schönen als das, was es ist" (129).

20. Ibid., 109.

21. Ibid., 110, emphasis added.

22. On this subject, see both J. Taminiaux, "Les Tensions internes de la *Critique du jugement,*" in *La Nostalgie de la Grèce à l'aube de l'idéalisme allemand. Kant et les Grecs dans l'itinéraire de Schiller, de Hölderlin et de Hegel* (The Hague: Martinus Nijhoff, 1967), 39; and P. Gambazzi, "La bellezza come non-oggetto e il suo soggetto," in *Azione e contemplazione* (Milan: IPL, 1992), 315.

23. Heidegger, *Nietzsche,* 1:109, emphases added.

24. See M. Heidegger, *Vom Wesen der Warheit* (Frankfurt am Main: Klostermann, 1943), §4; reprinted in M. Heidegger, *Wegmarken,* ed. F.-W. von Her-

rmann (Frankfurt am Main: Klostermann, 1976), where it is also explained that the "letting-be" does not mean indifference, but rather trusting in being, and letting oneself be enveloped by it.

25. See respectively Heidegger, *Being and Time,* §7b, 28ff.; and M. Heidegger, *Der Satz vom Grund* (Pfullingen: Günther Neske, 1957), 179. On the same subject, see also, in particular, the essay "Logos," in M. Heidegger, *Vorträge und Aufsätze* (Pfullingen: Günther Neske, 1954).

26. H. Arendt, *The Life of the Mind* (London: Secker and Warburg, 1978), 2:178.

27. See M. Heidegger, *Zur Erörterung der Gelassenheit: Aus einem Feldweggespräch über das Denken* (Pfullingen: Günther Neske, 1959), in *Gesamtausgabe,* vol. 13, *Aus der Erfahrung des Denkens 1910–1976* (Frankfurt am Main: Klostermann, 1983), 37–74; "Conversation on a Country Path about Thinking," in M. Heidegger, *Discourse on Thinking,* trans. John M. Anderson and E. Hans Freund (New York: Harper and Row, 1966), 58–90.

28. Heidegger, *Discourse on Thinking,* 75. The German says: "Das ist wieder dieses ruhelose Hin und Her zwischen Ja und Nein" (57).

29. David Michael Levin also develops a comparison between Heidegger and Merleau-Ponty that begins from the questions raised by the theme of *Gelassenheit* (see the provocative fifth chapter of his book *The Philosopher's Gaze: Modernity in the Shadows of Enlightenment,* 170–215). In the context of this comparison, Levin also emphasizes that, "unlike Merleau-Ponty, Heidegger always avoided the call to think through the problematic of embodiment" (204).

30. In Merleau-Ponty's use of the term, "feeling" is to be identified with "the primordial unconsciousness" (*RC* 179/199), with respect to which the *system* that incorporates the conscious and the unconscious is "a secondary formation." With regard to this latter system, it is worth noting that the first component—the conscious—dialectically recognizes its second component—the unconscious—by virtue of the fact that it *negates* it, according to Freud's text dedicated to "negation" (see S. Freud, "Die Verneinung," *Imago* 11, no. 3 [1925]: 217–21; "The Negation," trans. J. Strachey, in *The Standard Edition of the Complete Psychological Works of Sigmund Freud* [London: Hogarth, 1953–74], 19:235ff.). Freud's text elicited a comment by Jean Hyppolite that Merleau-Ponty seems to have been aware of (see *N* 351 n. 2/313 n. 14). In this comment, Hyppolite emphasizes how, for Freud, negating the repressed amounts to separating intellectual function from the emotional process. (Jean Hyppolite prepared the comment on Jacques Lacan's encouragement. See J. Hyppolite, "Commentaire parlé sur la 'Verneinung' de Freud" [1955], in *Figures de la pensée philosophique* [Paris: Presses Universitaires de France, 1971], 1:385–96.) On this basis, "the undividedness of feeling" of which Merleau-Ponty speaks could be seen too as an undividedness between the emotional and the intellectual.

31. In this sense, in the preparatory notes of the course devoted to "Cartesian Ontology and the Ontology of Today," Merleau-Ponty writes, as we know, that the "*derangement* of *all the senses*" celebrated by Rimbaud in the "Lettre du voyant" means to rediscover "not my thinking, but theirs" (*NC* 186). See note 24 of the previous chapter.

32. See H. Maldiney, *L'Art, l'éclair de l'être: Traversées* (Seyssel: Comp'Act, 1993), 333.

33. For more about feeling as letting-be, see the developments offered by R. Barbaras, *La Perception: Essai sur le sensible* (Paris: Hatier, 1994).

For more about the questions raised by our comparison between Heidegger's and Merleau-Ponty's conceptions of "letting-be," see Merleau-Ponty's course notes about "Heidegger: La philosophie comme problème," in NC 91–148. See also the commentary on these notes offered by F. Ciaramelli, "L'Originaire et l'immédiat: Remarques sur Heidegger et le dernier Merleau-Ponty," *Revue philosophique de Louvain* 96, no. 2 (May 1998): 198–231.

34. In this case, "to show" is the translation of the French expression *faire voir.*

35. "This is to be understood not as an imperfection . . . but as a philosophical *theme:* the incompleteness of the reduction . . . is not an obstacle to the reduction, it is the reduction itself, the rediscovery of vertical being.—" (*VI* 232/178).

36. In this regard, that work of creation, as Merleau-Ponty writes in a working note of *The Visible and the Invisible* significantly entitled "Philosophy and Literature," "is therefore a creation in a radical sense: a creation that is at the same time an adequation, the only way to obtain an adequation" (*VI* 251/197).

37. See chapter 2, "What Beginning of Knowledge?"

38. "Only the painter is entitled to look at everything without being obliged to appraise what he sees" (*OE* 14/123).

39. See *NC* 186ff./390–92, as well as "*Voyance*" in our previous chapter.

40. See also another often-quoted passage from *The Visible and the Invisible:* "[h]e who sees cannot possess the visible unless he is possessed by it, unless he *is of it*" (*VI* 177–78/134–35). This confirms, moreover, how (unlike Heidegger) Merleau-Ponty's problem does not lie in revoking every will to possess, but rather in recognizing the original and ineradicable reciprocity of possession. This same opinion is maintained by Barbaras: "Il n'y a pas d'alternative . . . entre saisir activement une chose et être dépossédé par elle" (Barbaras, "La Puissance du visible: Merleau-Ponty et Aristote," in *Le Tournant de l'expérience,* 19).

41. See *S* 228/181.

42. Christine Buci-Glucksmann, in particular, discusses the closeness between the aesthetic ontology of the later Merleau-Ponty and the ontological aesthetics of the baroque. See Buci- Glucksmann, *La Folie du voir,* esp. 73 and 85–86.

43. "There is no other meaning than carnal, figure and ground" (*VI* 319/265).

44. Arendt is a scholar who recognizes this deepest metaphorical origin of the concept. Significantly, in her discussion, she refers to the relationship of "symbolical exhibition" between ideas of reason and aesthetic ideas, outlined by Kant and defined in §59 of the *Critique of Judgment* (see "Language and Metaphor," in Arendt, *The Life of the Mind,* 1:98–110).

45. Barbaras also reaches this conclusion in the paragraph entitled "La Métaphorique du monde" of his *De l'être du phénomène: Sur l'ontologie de Merleau-Ponty* (Grenoble: Millon, 1991), 224ff. That paragraph provides a valid examina-

tion of the working note of *The Visible and the Invisible* dated November 26, 1959, which is devoted to the metaphor. Barbaras emphasizes how Merleau-Ponty criticizes the traditional conception of the metaphor as a simple transfer of sense from one entity to another. Along the same lines, see also J. Garelli, "Le Lieu d'un questionnement," *Les Cahiers de philosophie,* n.s., 7 (1989): 131–33.

46. M. Perniola, "Presentazione," in B. Gracián, *L'acutezza e l'arte dell'ingegno,* Italian trans. Giulia Poggi (Palermo: Aesthetica, 1986), 19; B. Gracián, *Agudeza y arte de ingenio* (1648).

47. See preface as well as chapter 1, note 35.

48. Perniola, "Presentazione," in *L'acutezza e l'arte dell'ingegno,* 19. See also the comparison between Merleau-Ponty and Gracián made by Buci-Glucksmann in *La Folie du voir,* 85.

Selected Bibliography

Texts on Merleau-Ponty

Barbaras, R. *De l'être du phénomène: Sur l'ontologie de Merleau-Ponty.* Grenoble: Millon, 1991.

———. *La Perception: Essai sur le sensible.* Paris: Hatier, 1994.

———. *Le Tournant de l'expérience: Recherches sur la philosophie de Merleau-Ponty.* Paris: Vrin, 1998.

———. "Phénoménalité et signification dans *Le visible et l'invisible.*" *Les Cahiers de philosophie,* n.s., no. 7 (1989): 25–53.

Barbaras, R., and P. Burke, coordinators. "Merleau-Ponty: From Nature to Ontology." *Chiasmi International,* n.s., 2 (2000).

Barbaras, R., ed. *Notes de cours sur "L'Origine de la géométrie" de Husserl* (by M. Merleau-Ponty) *suivi de recherches sur la phénoménologie de Merleau-Ponty.* Paris: Presses Universitaires de France, 1998.

Blanchot, M. "Le 'Discours philosophique.'" *L'Arc,* no. 46 (1971): 1–4.

Boehm, R. "Χιασμα: Merleau-Ponty und Heidegger." In *Durchblicke: Festschrift für Martin Heidegger zum 80. Geburtstag,* 350–68. Frankfurt am Main: Klostermann, 1970.

Bonan, R. *La Dimension commune.* 2 vols. Paris: L'Harmattan, 2001.

Bonomi, A. *Esistenza e struttura: Saggio su Merleau-Ponty.* Milan: Il Saggiatore, 1967.

Brena, G. L. *La struttura della percezione: Studio su Merleau-Ponty.* Milan: Vita e Pensiero, 1969.

Burke, P. "La creatività e l'inconscio in Merleau-Ponty e Schelling." *Chiasmi* 1 (1998): 51–75.

———. "Merleau-Ponty's Appropriation of Husserl's Notion of 'Präsenzfeld.'" In *Husserl in Contemporary Context,* ed. B. C. Hopkins, 37–58. Dordrecht: Kluwer Academic Publishers, 1997.

Burke, P., and J. van der Veken, eds. *Merleau-Ponty in Contemporary Perspective.* Dordrecht: Kluwer Academic Publishers, 1993.

Busch, T. W., and S. Gallagher, eds. *Merleau-Ponty, Hermeneutics, and Postmodernism.* Albany: State University of New York Press, 1992.

Calabrò, D. *L'infanzia della filosofia: Saggio sulla filosofia dell'educazione di Maurice Merleau-Ponty.* Turin: UTET, 2002.

Capalbo, C. "L'Historicité chez Merleau-Ponty." *Revue philosophique de Louvain,* 73 (1975): 511–35.

Carbone, M. *Ai confini dell'esprimibile: Merleau-Ponty a partire da Cézanne e da Proust.* 2d ed. Milan: Guerini e Associati, 1995.

———. *Di alcuni motivi in Marcel Proust.* Milan: Cortina, 1998.

———. "Il Cézanne dei filosofi francesi: Da Merleau-Ponty a Deleuze." In *Il Cézanne degli scrittori, dei poeti e dei filosofi,* ed. G. Cianci, E. Franzini, and A. Negri, 243–62. Milan: Bocca, 2001.

———. *Il sensibile e l'eccedente: Mondo estetico, arte, pensiero.* Milan: Guerini e Associati, 1996.

———. "La parola dell'àugure: Merleau-Ponty e la 'filosofia del freudismo.'" In *Figure del feticismo,* ed. S. Mistura, 262–91. Turin: Einaudi, 2001.

———. *La Visibilité de l'invisible: Merleau-Ponty entre Cézanne et Proust.* Hildesheim: Georg Olms, 2001.

———, coordinator. "Merleau-Ponty: Figures and Grounds of the Flesh." *Chiasmi International,* n.s., 4 (2002).

———, coordinator. "Merleau-Ponty: The Contemporary Heritage." *Chiasmi International,* n.s., 1 (1999).

Carbone, M., and C. Fontana, eds. *Negli specchi dell'essere: Saggi sulla filosofia di Merleau-Ponty,* Cernusco Lombardone: Hestia, 1993.

Carmelo Rosa Renaud, I. *Communication et expression chez Merleau-Ponty.* Lisbon: Universidade Nova de Lisboa, 1985.

Castoriadis, C. "Le dicible et l'indicible." *L'Arc,* no. 46 (1971): 67–79.

Charcosset, J.-P. *Merleau-Ponty: Approches phénoménologiques.* Paris: Hachette, 1981.

Ciaramelli, F. "L'Originaire et l'immédiat: Remarques sur Heidegger et le dernier Merleau-Ponty." *Revue philosophique de Louvain* 96, no. 2 (May 1998): 198–231.

Compton, J. J. "Merleau-Ponty's Metaphorical Philosophy." *Research in Phenomenology* 23 (1993–94): 221–26.

Costantino, S. *La testimonianza del linguaggio: Saggio su Merleau-Ponty.* Milan: FrancoAngeli, 1999.

Dastur, F. *Chair et langage: Essais sur Merleau-Ponty.* La Versanne: Encre Marine, 2001.

Davis, D. H., ed. *Merleau-Ponty's Later Works and Their Practical Implications: The Dehiscence of Responsibility.* Amherst, N.Y.: Humanity Books, 2001.

Deguy, M. "Le Visible et l'invisible." *La Nouvelle Revue française,* no. 138 (1964): 1062–72.

Derossi, G. *Maurice Merleau-Ponty.* Turin: Edizioni di "Filosofia," 1965.

Dillon, M. C. *Merleau-Ponty's Ontology.* 2d ed. Evanston: Northwestern University Press, 1997.

———, ed. *Merleau-Ponty Vivant.* Albany: State University of New York Press, 1991.

Duchene, J. "La Structure de la phénoménalisation dans la *Phénoménologie de la perception* de Merleau-Ponty." *Revue de métaphysique et de morale* 83, no. 3 (1978): 373–98. English translation by J. Donceel (with extensive revisions by the editor) as "The Structure of Phenomenalization in the *Phenomenology of Perception* of Merleau-Ponty." In *Merleau-Ponty: Critical Essays,* ed. Henry Pietersma, 45–75. Washington, D.C.: Center for Advanced Research in Phenomenology and University Press of America, 1989.

Dufrenne, M. "Maurice Merleau-Ponty." *Les Études philosophiques,* no. 1 (1962): 81–92.

Dupond, P. "Temps, nature et histoire dans la *Phénoménologie de la perception.*" *Etudes phénoménologiques,* nos. 31–32 (2000): 3–33.

Edie, J. M. "Was Merleau-Ponty a Structuralist?" *Semiotica* 4, no. 4 (1971): 297–323.

Evans, F., and L. Lawlor, eds. *Chiasms: Merleau-Ponty's Notion of Flesh.* Albany: State University of New York Press, 2000.

Flynn, B. "Merleau-Ponty and Benjamin: Language/Loss/Restoration." *Etudes phénoménologiques,* nos. 31–32 (2000): 67–81.

Fontaine-de Visscher, L. *Phénomène ou structure? Essai sur le langage chez Merleau-Ponty.* Brussels: Publications des Facultés universitaires Saint-Louis, 1974.

Foti, V. M., ed. *Merleau-Ponty: Difference, Materiality, Painting.* Atlantic Highlands, N.J.: Humanities, 1996.

Franzini, E. "Merleau-Ponty, Husserl e la natura." *Chiasmi* 1 (1998): 91–95.

Froman, W. J. "Merleau-Ponty and Phenomenological Philosophy." *Etudes phénoménologiques* nos. 31–32 (2000): 83–101.

———. *Merleau-Ponty: Language and the Act of Speech.* East Brunswick: Associated University Press, 1982.

Gambazzi, P. "Fenomenologia e psicoanalisi nell'ultimo Merleau-Ponty." *Aut Aut,* n.s., nos. 232–33 (July–October 1989): 105–29.

———. "La piega e il pensiero: Sull'ontologia di Merleau-Ponty." *Aut Aut,* n.s., nos. 262–63 (July–October 1994): 21–47.

———. "Monadi, pieghe e specchi: Sul leibnizianesimo di Merleau-Ponty e Deleuze." *Chiasmi* 1 (1998): 27–50.

Garelli, J. "Le lieu d'un questionnement." *Les Cahiers de philosophie,* n.s., no. 7 (1989): 107–43.

George, F. "Merleau-Ponty: La première vue et l'être pour X." *Critique* 37, nos. 409–10 (June–July 1981): 567–77.

Geraets, T. F. *Vers une nouvelle philosophie transcendentale: La genèse de la philosophie de M. Merleau-Ponty jusqu'à la "Phénoménologie de la perception."* The Hague: Martinus Nijhoff, 1971.

Giuliani-Tagmann, R. *Sprache und Erfahrung in den Schriften von Merleau-Ponty.* Bern: Peter Lang, 1983.

Grathoff, R., and W. Sprondel, eds. *Maurice Merleau-Ponty und das Problem der Struktur in den Sozialwissenschaften.* Stuttgart: Ferdinand Enke, 1976.

Gregori, I. *Merleau-Pontys Phänomenologie der Sprache.* Heidelberg: Carl Winter, 1977.

Heidsieck, F. *L'Ontologie de Merleau-Ponty.* Paris: Presses Universitaires de France, 1971.

———, ed. "Merleau-Ponty: Le philosophe et son langage." *Recherches sur la philosophie et le langage,* no. 15 (1993).

Hyppolite, J. *Figures de la pensée philosophique: Écrits (1931–1968),* 2:685–758. Paris: Presses Universitaires de France, 1971.

Invitto, G. *Merleau-Ponty e la filosofia come vigilanza.* Lecce: Milella, 1981.

———, ed. *Merleau-Ponty: filosofia, esistenza politica.* Naples: Guida, 1982.

Irigaray, L. "L'Invisible de la chair. Lecture de Merleau-Ponty, *Le Visible et l'invisible,* 'L'entrelacs-le chiasme.'" In *Éthique de la différence sexuelle.* Paris: Minuit, 1984.

Johnson, G., ed. *The Merleau-Ponty Aesthetics Reader: Philosophy and Painting.* Evanston: Northwestern University Press, 1993.

Kaufmann, P. "De la vision picturale au désir de peindre." *Critique* 20, no. 211 (December 1964): 1046–64.

Klein, R. "Peinture moderne et phénoménologie." *Critique* 19, no. 191 (April 1963): 336–53.

Kwant, R. C. *From Phenomenology to Metaphysics: An Inquiry into the Last Period of Merleau-Ponty's Philosophical Life.* Pittsburgh and Louvain: Duquesne University Press and Nauwelaerts, 1966.

———. *The Phenomenological Philosophy of Merleau-Ponty.* Pittsburgh and Louvain: Duquesne University Press and Nauwelaerts, 1963.

Landgrebe, L. *Merleau-Pontys Auseinandersetzung mit Husserls Phänomenologie.* In *Phänomenologie und Geschichte,* 167–81. Gütersloh: Gütersloher Verlagshaus Gerd Mohn, 1968.

Lawlor, L., coordinator. "Merleau-Ponty: Non-Philosophy and Philosophy." *Chiasmi International,* n.s., 3 (2001).

Lefeuvre, M. *Merleau-Ponty au delà de la phénoménologie.* Paris: Klincksieck, 1976.

Lefort, C. "D'un doute à l'autre." *Esprit,* no. 66 (June 1982): 23–30.

———. "Philosophie et non-philosophie." *Esprit,* no. 66 (June 1982): 101–12.

———. "Postface" to M. Merleau-Ponty, *Le Visible et l'invisible,* 337–60. Paris: Gallimard, 1964. English translation as "Editor's Foreword," in M. Merleau-Ponty, *The Visible and the Invisible,* trans. Alphonso Lingis, xi–xxxiii. Evanston: Northwestern University Press, 1968.

———. "Préface" to M. Merleau-Ponty, *Notes des cours au Collège de France 1958–1959 et 1960–1961,* ed. Stéphanie Ménasé, 7–30. Paris: Gallimard, 1996.

———. "Présentation" to M. Merleau-Ponty, "Philosophie et non-philosophie depuis Hegel." In M. Merleau-Ponty, *Notes des cours au Collège de France 1958–1959 et 1960–1961,* 272–73.

———. *Sur une colonne absente. Ecrits autour de Merleau-Ponty.* Paris: Gallimard, 1978.

Lévinas, E. "De l'intersubjectivité: Notes sur Merleau-Ponty." In E. Lévinas, *Hors sujet,* 143–53. Montpellier: Fata Morgana, 1978.

Lingis, A. *Libido: The French Existential Theories.* Bloomington: Indiana University Press, 1985.

Lisciani-Petrini, E. *La passione del mondo: Saggio su Merleau-Ponty.* Naples: Edizioni Scientifiche Italiane, 2002.

———. "Merleau-Ponty–Bergson: Un dialogo 'se faisant.'" *Il pensiero,* n.s., no. 33 (1993): 67–93.

Madison, G. B. *La Phénoménologie de Merleau-Ponty: Une recherche des limites de la conscience.* Paris: Klincksieck, 1973. English version as *The Phenomenology of Merleau-Ponty.* Athens: Ohio University Press, 1981.

Mallin, S. B. *Merleau-Ponty's Philosophy.* New Haven and London: Yale University Press, 1979.

Mancini, S. "Il narcisismo della carne: Merleau-Ponty e l'interpretazione ontologica della pittura." *Aut Aut,* n.s., nos. 202–3 (July–October 1984): 136–48.

———. "L'assoluto dialettico in Merleau-Ponty." *Il centauro,* no. 10 (1984): 90–110.

———. *Sempre di nuovo: Merleau-Ponty e la dialettica dell'espressione.* 2d ed. Milan: Mimesis, 2001.

Marinotti, A. *Percezione e conoscenza: Linee della fenomenologia genetica di M. Merleau-Ponty.* Florence: Alfani, 1983.

Matos Dias, I. *Merleau-Ponty: Une poïétique du sensible.* Toulouse: Presses Universitaires du Mirail, 2001.

Melle, U. *Das Wahrnehmungsproblem und seine Verwandlung in phänomenologischer Einstellung: Untersuchungen zu den phänomenologischen Wahrnehmungstheorien von Husserl, Gurwitsch und Merleau-Ponty.* The Hague and Boston: Lancaster and Martinus Nijhoff, 1983.

Moiso, F. "Una ragione all'altezza della natura: La convergenza fra Schelling e Merleau-Ponty." *Chiasmi* 1 (1998): 83–90.

Neri, G. D., ed. "Merleau-Ponty: Figure della nuova ontologia." *Aut Aut,* n.s., nos. 232–33 (July–October 1989).

O'Neill, J. *The Communicative Body: Studies in Communicative Philosophy, Politics, and Sociology.* Evanston: Northwestern University Press, 1989.

Paci, E. "Introduzione" to M. Merleau-Ponty, *Elogio della filosofia,* Italian translation by Enzo Paci, V–XL. Turin: Paravia, 1958. Reprinted in *Chiasmi International,* n.s., 2 (2000): 19–34.

———. "Introduzione" to M. Merleau-Ponty, *Senso e non senso,* Italian translation by Paolo Caruso, 9–18. Milan: Il Saggiatore, 1962.

Papi, F. "Merleau-Ponty scrittore dell'essere." *Segni e comprensione,* no. 44 (September–December 2001): 32–37.

Pietersma, H., ed. *Merleau-Ponty: Critical Essays.*Washington, D.C.: Center for Advanced Research in Phenomenology and University Press of America, 1989.

Puech, C. "Merleau-Ponty: La Langue, le sujet et l'institué: La linguistique dans la philosophie." *Langages,* no. 77 (March 1985): 21–32.

Ramírez Cobián, M. T. *Cuerpo y arte: Para una estética merleaupontiana.* Mexico: UAEM, 1996.

Richir, M. "La Défenestration." *L'Arc,* no. 46 (1971): 31–42.

———. "Merleau-Ponty: Un Tout Nouveau Rapport à la psychanalyse." *Les Cahiers de philosophie,* n.s., no. 7 (1989): 155–87.

Richir, M., and É. Tassin, eds. *Merleau-Ponty: Phénoménologie et expériences.* Grenoble: Millon, 1992.

Ricoeur, P. "Par-delà Husserl et Heidegger." *Les Cahiers de philosophie,* n.s., no. 7 (1989): 17–23.

Robinet, A. *Merleau-Ponty: Sa vie, son oeuvre.* Paris: Presses Universitaires de France, 1963.

Russon, J. "Embodiment and Responsibility: Merleau-Ponty and the Ontology of Nature." *Man and World* 24 (1994): 291–308.

Semerari, G. *Da Schelling a Merleau-Ponty: Studi sulla filosofia contemporanea.* Bologna: Cappelli, 1962.

Sichère, B. *Merleau-Ponty ou le corps de la philosophie.* Paris: Grasset, 1982.

Silverman, H. J., ed. *Philosophy and Non-Philosophy Since Merleau-Ponty.* New York and London: Routledge, 1988.

Simon, A. and N. Castin (eds.), *Merleau-Ponty et le littéraire.* Paris: Presses de l'École normale supérieure, 1997.

Slatman, J. *L'Expression au-delà de la représentation: Sur l'aisthêsis et l'esthétique chez Merleau-Ponty.* Amsterdam: Academisch Proefschrift Universiteit van Amsterdam, 2001.

Sordini, A. "I simboli e il corpo: Merleau-Ponty filosofo dell'espressione." *Fenomenologia e società,* no. 7 (1985): 67–86.

Strasser, S. "Merleau-Ponty et 'Le Métaphysique dans l'homme.'" *Etudes phénoménologiques* 4, no. 7 (1988): 145–65.

Taminiaux, J. "La Phénoménologie dans le dernier ouvrage de Merleau-Ponty." In *Le Regard et l'excédent,* 72–89. The Hague: Martinus Nijhoff, 1977. English translation by Alphonso Lingis and James Decker as "Phenomenology in Merleau-Ponty's Late Work." In J. Taminiaux, *Dialectic and Difference: Modern Thought and the Sense of Human Limits,* ed. and trans. Robert Crease and James T. Decker, 115–29. Atlantic Highlands, N.J.: Humanities, 1985.

———. "Le Penseur et le peintre: Sur Merleau-Ponty." *La Part de l'oeil,* no. 7 (1991): 39–46. English translation by Michael Gendre as "The Thinker and the Painter." In *Merleau-Ponty Vivant,* ed. Martin C. Dillon, 195–211. Albany: State University of New York Press, 1991.

———. "L'Expérience, l'expression et la forme dans l'itinéraire de Merleau-Ponty." In *Le Regard et l'excédent,* 90–115. English translation by James Decker as "Experience, Expression, and Form in Merleau-Ponty's Itinerary." In *Dialectic and Difference,* 131–54.

———. "Merleau-Ponty de la dialectique à l'hyperdialectique." In *Recoupements,* 91–117. Brussels: Ousia, 1982. English translation by Robert Crease as "Merleau-Ponty: From Dialectic to Hyperdialectic." In *Dialectic and Difference,* 155–72.

Thierry, Y. *Du corps parlant: Le langage chez Merleau-Ponty.* Brussels: Ousia, 1987.

Tilliette, X. "L'Esthétique de Merleau-Ponty." *Rivista di estetica,* no. 1 (1969): 102–19.

———. *Merleau-Ponty ou la mesure de l'homme.* Paris: Seghers, 1970.

Toadvine, T., and L. Embree, eds. *Merleau-Ponty's Reading of Husserl.* Dordrecht: Kluwer Academic Publishers, 2002.

Tymieniecka, A.-T., ed. *Merleau-Ponty, le psychique et le corporel.* Paris: Aubier, 1988.

Vanzago, L. *Modi del tempo: Simultaneità, processualità, relazionalità tra Whitehead e Merleau-Ponty.* Milan: Mimesis, 2001.

Villela-Petit, M. "'Qui voit?' Du privilège de la peinture chez Maurice Merleau-Ponty." *Les Études philosophiques,* no. 2 (April–June 2001): 261–78.

Waelhens, A (de). *Une Philosophie de l'ambiguïté: L'existentialisme de M. Merleau-Ponty.* 4th ed. Louvain: Publications Universitaires de Louvain, 1970.

Waldenfels, B. "Vérité à faire." *Les Cahiers de philosophie,* n.s., no. 7 (1989): 55–68.

Waldenfels, B., and R. Giuliani. "Turbine del tempo: Il tema del tempo in Merleau-Ponty." *Segni e comprensione,* no. 44 (September–December 2001): 38–58.

Zamboni, C. "Ermeneutica della scrittura o iniziazione attraverso il testo?" *Aut Aut,* n.s., nos. 202–3 (July–October 1984): 161–71.

Other Texts

Abram, D. *The Spell of the Sensuous: Perception and Language in a More-than-Human World.* New York: Pantheon Books, 1996.

Agamben, G. *Infanzia e storia: Distruzione dell'esperienza e origine della storia.* 2d ed. Turin: Einaudi, 1979.

Arendt, H. *The Life of the Mind.* 2 vols. London: Secker and Warburg, 1978.

Beaufret, J. *De l'existentialisme à Heidegger: Introduction aux philosophies de l'existence.* Paris: Vrin, 1986.

Benjamin, W. "Über einige Motive bei Baudelaire" (1939–40). In W. Benjamin, *Gesammelte Schriften,* vol. 1, bk. 2, ed. R. Tiedemann and H. Schweppenhäuser, 605–53. Frankfurt am Main: Suhrkamp, 1972–77. English translation by Harry Zohn as "On Some Motifs in Baudelaire." In W. Benjamin, *Illuminations,* 155–200. New York: Schocken Books, 1968.

———. "Zum Bilde Prousts" (1929). In W. Benjamin, *Gesammelte Schriften,* vol. 2, bk. 1, ed. R. Tiedemann and H. Schweppenhäuser, 310–25. Frankfurt am Main: Suhrkamp, 1972–77. English translation as "The Image of Proust." In *Illuminations,* 201–15.

Bernet, R. *La Vie du sujet: Recherches sur l'interprétation de Husserl dans la phénoménologie.* Paris: Presses Universitaires de France, 1994.

Blumenberg, H. *Das Lachen der Thrakerin: Eine Urgeschichte der Theorie.* Frankfurt am Main: Suhrkamp, 1987.

Buci-Glucksmann, C. *La Folie du voir: De l'esthétique baroque.* Paris: Galilée, 1986.

Buytendijk, F. "Les Différences essentielles des fonctions psychiques chez l'homme et les animaux." *Cahiers de philosophie de la nature* 4 (1930).

Charbonnier, G. *Le Monologue du peintre I.* Paris: Julliard, 1959.

Claudel, P. *L'Oeil écoute.* Paris: Gallimard, 1946.

Comolli, G. "Il paese della felicità dolente: Sul 'sapere precario' di Proust." *Aut Aut,* n.s., nos. 182–83 (March–June 1981): 31–44.

Dauenhauer, B. P. *Silence: The Phenomenon and Its Ontological Significance.* Bloomington: Indiana University Press, 1980.

Deleuze, G. *Marcel Proust et les signes.* 7th ed. Paris: Presses Universitaires de France, 1987.

Deleuze, G., and F. Guattari. *Qu'est-ce que la philosophie?* Paris: Minuit, 1991.

Descartes, R. *Oeuvres philosophiques,* ed. F. Alquié, vol. 1. Paris: Bordas, 1998.

Descombes, V. *Le Même et l'autre: Quarante-cinq ans de philosophie française (1933–1978).* Paris: Minuit, 1979.

———. *Proust: Philosophie du roman.* Paris: Minuit, 1987.

Fink, E. "Die phänomenologische Philosophie Edmund Husserls in der gegenwärtingen Kritik." *Kant-Studien* 37, nos. 3–4 (1933). In E. Fink, *Studien zur Phänomenologie.* The Hague: Martinus Nijhoff, 1966.

Florival, G. *Le Désir chez Proust: A la recherche du sens.* Louvain, Paris: Nauwelaerts, 1971.

Freud, S. "Die Verneinung." *Imago* 11, no. 3 (1925): 217–21. English translation by J. Strachey as "The Negation." In *The Standard Edition of the Complete Psychological Works of Sigmund Freud,* 19:235ff. London: Hogarth, 1953–74.

Gambazzi, G. "La bellezza come non-oggetto e il suo soggetto." In *Azione e contemplazione,* 293–326. Milan: IPL, 1992.

———. *L'occhio e il suo inconscio.* Milan: Cortina, 1999.

Garelli, J. *Introduction au logos du monde esthétique: De la* chôra *platonicienne au schématisme transcendantal et à l'expérience phénoménologique de l'être-au-monde.* Paris: Beauchesne, 2000.

———. *Rythmes et mondes: Au revers de l'identité et de l'alterité.* Grenoble: Millon, 1991.

Genette, G. *Proust et le langage indirect.* In G. Genette, *Figures II,* 223–94. Paris: Seuil, 1969.

Hegel, G. W. F. *Enzyklopädie der philosophischen Wissenschaften im Grundrisse* (1830). English translation by T. F. Geraets, W. A. Suchting, and H. S. Harris as *The Encyclopaedia Logic: Part I of the Encyclopaedia of Philosophical Sciences with the Zusatze.* Indianapolis: Hackett, 1991.

———. *Phänomenologie des Geistes* (1807). English translation by A. V. Miller as *Hegel's Phenomenology of Spirit.* New York: Oxford University Press, 1977.

Heidegger, M. *Brief über den Humanismus* (1947). French translation by Roger Munier as *Lettre sur l'humanisme.* Bilingual edition. Paris: Aubier-Montaigne, 1964.

———. *Der Satz vom Grund.* Pfullingen: Günther Neske, 1957.

———. *Gelassenheit.* Pfullingen: Günther Neske, 1959. English translation by John M. Anderson and E. Hans Freund as *Discourse on Thinking.* New York: Harper and Row, 1966.

———. *Hegels Begriff der Erfahrung* (1942–43). In M. Heidegger, *Holzwege,* 105–92. Frankfurt am Main: Klostermann, 1950. English translation as *Hegel's Concept of Experience (with a Section from Hegel's "Phenomenology of Spirit" in the Kenley Royce Dove Translation).* New York: Harper and Row, 1970.

———. *Nietzsche.* 2 vols. Pfullingen: Günther Neske, 1961. English translation by David Farrell Krell as *Nietzsche.* 4 vols. New York: Harper and Row, 1979–87.

———. *Sein und Zeit* (1927). 10th ed. Tübingen: Max Niemeyer, 1963. English translation by Joan Stambaugh as *Being and Time.* Albany: State University of New York Press, 1996.

———. *Unterwegs zur Sprache.* Pfullingen: Günther Neske, 1959.

———. *Vorträge und Aufsätze.* Pfullingen: Günther Neske, 1954.

———. *Wegmarken,* ed. F.-W. von Herrmann. Frankfurt am Main: Klostermann, 1976.

Herr, L. "Hegel." In *Choix d'écrits,* 2:109–46. Paris: Presses Universitaires de France, 1932.

Husserl, E. *Cartesianische Meditationen und Pariser Vorträge,* ed. S. Strasser. In *Husserliana,* vol. 1. The Hague: Martinus Nijhoff, 1950.

———. *Die Krisis der europäischen Wissenschaften und die transzendentale Phänomenologie,* ed. W. Biemel. In *Husserliana,* vol. 6. The Hague: Martinus Nijhoff, 1954.

———. *Formale und transzendentale Logik: Versuch einer Kritik der logischen Vernunft* (1929), ed. P. Janssen. In *Husserliana,* vol. 17. The Hague: Martinus Nijhoff, 1974.

———. *Ideen zu einer reinen Phänomenologie und phänomenologischen Philosophie,* bk.2, *Phänomenologische Untersuchungen zur Konstitution,* ed. M. Biemel. In *Husserliana,* vol. 4. The Hague: Martinus Nijhoff, 1952.

———. "Umsturz der kopernikanischen Lehre in der gewöhnlichen weltanschaulichen Interpretation. Die Ur-Arche Erde bewegt sich nicht. Grundlegende Untersuchungen zum phänomenologischen Ursprung der Körperlichkeit, der Räumlichkeit der Natur im ersten naturwissenschaftlichen Sinne" (May 7–9, 1934). In *Philosophical Essays in Memory of Edmund Husserl,* ed. Marvin Farber, 307–25. Cambridge: Harvard University Press, 1940. English translation by Fred Kersten as "Foundational Investigations of the Phenomenological Origin of the Spatiality of Nature." In E. Husserl, *Shorter Works,* ed. Peter McCormick and Frederick A. Elliston, 222–33. Notre Dame: University of Notre Dame Press and Harvester Press, 1981.

———. *Zur Phänomenologie des inneren Zeitbewusstsein (1893–1917),* ed. R. Boehm. In *Husserliana,* vol. 10. The Hague: Martinus Nijhoff, 1966. English translation by John Brough as *On the Phenomenology of the Consciousness of Internal Time.* Dordrecht: Kluwer Academic Publishers, 1991.

Hyppolite, J. "Commentaire parlé sur la 'Verneinung' de Freud" (1955). In J. Hyppolite, *Figures de la pensée philosophique: Écrits (1931–1968),* 1:385–96. Paris: Presses Universitaires de France, 1971.

———. *Genèse et structure de la "Phénoménologie de l'esprit" de Hegel.* 2 vols. Paris: Aubier- Montaigne, 1946. English translation by Samuel Cherniak and John Heckman as *Genesis and Structure of Hegel's "Phenomenology of Spirit."* Evanston: Northwestern University Press, 1974.

Kant, I. *Kritik der Urteilskraft* (1790). English translation by J. H. Bernard as *The Critique of Judgment.* Amherst, N.Y.: Prometheus Books, 2000.

Klee, P. *Das bildnerische Denken.* Basel: Benno Schwabe, 1956.

Levin, D. M. *The Philosopher's Gaze: Modernity in the Shadows of Enlightenment.* Berkeley and Los Angeles: University of California Press, 1999.

Lyotard, J.-F. *Discours, figure.* 3rd ed. Paris: Klincksieck, 1978.

———. "Freud selon Cézanne." In J.-F. Lyotard, *Des dispositifs pulsionnels,* 71–94. Paris: Union Générale d'Editions, 1973.

———. "La Philosophie et la peinture à l'ère de leur expérimentation: Contribution à une idée de la postmodernité." *Rivista di estetica,* no. 9 (1981): 3–15. English translation by Maria Minich Brewer and Daniel Brewer as "Philosophy and Painting in the Age of Their Experimentation: Contribution to an Idea of Postmodernity." In *The Merleau-Ponty Aesthetics Reader,* ed. Galen Johnson, 323–35. Evanston: Northwestern University Press, 1993.

Maldiney, H. *L'Art, l'éclair de l'être: Traversées.* Seyssel: Comp'Act, 1993.

Nancy, J.-L. *Corpus.* 2d ed. Paris: Métailié, 2000.

———. *The Birth to Presence,* trans. Brian Holmes et al. Stanford: Stanford University Press, 1993.

Paci, E. *Funzione delle scienze e significato dell'uomo.* Milan: Il Saggiatore, 1963.

Pascal, B. *Pascal's Pensées* (1669). Bilingual edition. English translation by H. F. Stewart. London: Routledge and Kegan Paul, 1950.

Perniola, M. "Presentazione" to B. Gracián, *L'acutezza e l'arte dell'ingegno,* Italian translation by Giulia Poggi. Palermo: Aesthetica, 1986. B. Gracián, *Agudeza y arte de ingenio.* 1648.

Proust, M. *A la recherche du temps perdu,* ed. Pierre Clarac and André Ferré. 3 vols. Bibliothèque de la Pléiade. Paris: Gallimard, 1954. English translation as *Remembrance of Things Past,* vol. 1 (trans. C. K. Scott-Moncrieff and Terence Kilmartin), vol. 2 (trans. C. K. Scott-Moncrieff and Terence Kilmartin), vol. 3 (trans. C. K. Scott-Moncrieff, Terence Kilmartin, and Andreas Mayor). New York: Vintage, 1981.

———. *"Contre Sainte-Beuve" précédé de "Pastiches et mélanges" et suivi de "Essais et articles,"* edited by Pierre Clarac with the collaboration of Yves Sandre. Bibliothèque de la Pléiade. Paris: Gallimard, 1971.

———. *Correspondance générale.* Vol. 3. Paris: Plon, 1932.

Rella, F. *Il silenzio e le parole: Il pensiero nel tempo della crisi.* Milan: Feltrinelli, 1981.

Richir, M. *Phénomènes, temps et êtres: Ontologie et phénoménologie.* Grenoble: Millon, 1987.

Ricoeur, P. *La Mémoire, l'histoire, l'oubli.* Paris: Seuil, 2000.

———. "Langage (Philosophie)." In *Encyclopaedia Universalis,* 9:771–81. Paris: 1971.

———. *Temps et récit.* Vol. 2, *La Configuration dans le récit de fiction.* Paris: Seuil, 1984. English translation by Kathleen McLaughlin and David Pellaue as *Time and Narrative,* vol. 2. Chicago: University of Chicago Press, 1985.

Rimbaud, A. *Complete Works, Selected Letters,* ed. W. Folie. Chicago and London: The University of Chicago Press, 1966.

Ronchi, R. *Bergson filosofo dell'interpretazione.* Genoa: Marietti, 1990.

Silverman, H. J. *Inscriptions: After Phenomenology and Structuralism.* 2d ed. Evanston: Northwestern University Press, 1997.

Sini, C. *Il silenzio e la parola.* Genoa: Marietti, 1989.

Spiegelberg, H. *The Phenomenological Movement: A Historical Introduction.* 3rd rev. and enl. ed. The Hague: Martinus Nijhoff, 1982.

Taminiaux, J. *La Nostalgie de la Grèce à l'aube de l'idéalisme allemand: Kant et les Grecs dans l'itinéraire de Schiller, de Hölderlin et de Hegel.* The Hague: Martinus Nijhoff, 1967.

Uexküll, J. von. *Streifzüge durch die Umwelten von Tieren und Menschen. Ein Bilderbuch unsichtbarer Welten.* Berlin: Springer, 1934. Italian translation by Paola Manfredi as *Ambiente e comportamento,* with an "Introduzione" by Felice Mondella. Milan: Il Saggiatore, 1967.

———. *Umwelt und Innenwelt der Tiere.* Berlin: Springer, 1909.

Waldenfels, B. *Phänomenologie in Frankreich.* Frankfurt am Main: Suhrkamp, 1983.

Wertheimer, M. *Productive Thinking.* New York and London: Harper and Brothers, 1945.

Index

About the Author

Mauro Carbone holds the Chair of Aesthetics at the State University of Milan in Italy and is the author of essays and books on Merleau-Ponty. He is highly regarded throughout Europe principally as a major scholar in phenomenological and postphenomenological thought but also as a translator and an editor. He is a founding member of the Italian Merleau-Ponty Society and the editor of the journal *Chiasmi International: Trilingual Studies concerning the Thought of Merleau-Ponty*.

Consulting Editors

Robert Bernasconi
Judith P. Butler
David Carr
Edward S. Casey
Stanley Cavell
Roderick M. Chisholm
Hubert L. Dreyfus
Lester E. Embree
Dagfinn Føllesdal
Véronique Fóti
Irene Harvey
Dieter Henrich
Don Ihde
†Emmanuel Levinas
Alphonso Lingis
William McBride
J. N. Mohanty
†Maurice Natanson
Graeme Nicholson
Frederick Olafson
Paul Ricoeur
Tom Rockmore
George Schrader
Calvin O. Schrag
Thomas Sheehan
Hugh J. Silverman
Robert Sokolowski
†Herbert Spiegelberg
Charles Taylor
Samuel J. Todes
Bruce W. Wilshire
David Wood